"Many Christian resources focus either on biblical study to the neglect of deep personal life transformation or on life application based on a very flattened understanding of the gospel. World Harvest has drawn upon their history of rich gospel-based training to produce a series that targets real-life transformation grounded in a robust, grace-based theology. Only a resource saturated in the gospel can lead to the kind of meaningful life change promised to us in the Bible, and I am thrilled to see such a resource now available."

    Rev. David H. Kim, Director of the Gotham Initiative, Redeemer Presbyterian Church, NYC

"I love the series of small group resources, *Gospel Identity*, *Gospel Growth*, and *Gospel Love*. They are theologically rich, but not stuffy; practical, but not pragmatic. They are life-transforming resources that will be used to transform communities on a mission with the gospel."

    Scott Thomas, Pastor of Pastoral Development, The Journey Church

"*Gospel Identity* is a rich, interactive analysis of our deepest self in relation to the gospel. The lessons are weighty and deep because the writers have a panoramic and majestic view of the gospel. Complex gospel content is brought into focus through several helpful charts and diagrams, which are obviously the fruit of years of gospel discipleship. This is not just gospel information; this is deep gospel application that is practical and specific, so that gospel encouragement translates into a lifestyle of witness and love. The participant is constantly encouraged toward gospel relationship with others and each section leads into individual and group prayer. The issue is identity, but the study doesn't stop at introspection. Gospel renewal leads to sharing the radical news of our union with Christ by faith and caring for those around us."

    John Smed, Director, Prayer Current Ministries

"This study brings a powerful experience of gospel truth and a personal relationship with Jesus and all those that he has placed in your life. Using biblical truths, written to open the eyes of all hearts to sins, and full of challenges by the Holy Spirit to change and grow, this is the study you need. User-friendly, even for a first time leader, it is progressive, time-sensitive, and will invite the most timid participant into heart application. I highly recommend this to all who are committed to growing closer to God and being a gospel tool to help others."

    Nancy Puryear, Women's ministry director (more than eleven years), Christ Community Church; cross-cultural counselor

"God used Jack Miller to help Christians, and pastors especially, to recover the gospel of Jesus Christ as the functional core of the Christian faith. Jack's famous line, 'Cheer up, you're worse off than you think,' re-opened the door to many of us with an invitation to drop the pretense of a good life and to admit and delight in our continuing, desperate need for Jesus. As a church planter and trainer of church planters, I have often wished for a concise series of Bible studies that would help churches to not only know this gospel of grace, but to experience it as well. That's precisely what this series of gospel studies offers. It is a great way to biblically and relationally ground Christians in the gospel of Jesus Christ, and I heartily recommend it."

John F. Thomas, PhD, Director of Global Training, Redeemer City to City

"I'm probably the most 'religious' person you know. I make my living teaching religious students (in seminary) to be more religious, doing religious broadcasts, writing religious books, and preaching religious sermons. It's very easy to lose the 'main thing' about the Christian faith in a religious morass. These studies remind me that it's all about Jesus, and Jesus is all about the Good News (the gospel). They are refreshing, informative, and life changing. In fact, these studies are like a refreshing drink of cold, pure water to a thirsty man. Read and use these books from World Harvest Mission and get out of the way as you listen to the laughter and relief of the redeemed."

Steve Brown, Key Life radio broadcaster; author of *Three Free Sins: God Isn't Mad at You*

"*Gospel Identity* is unique in that it works at the very heart of our faith. It is a marriage course, a discipleship course, and a Bible study, but it is so much more. It is all about getting the central passion of Christianity—the cross of Jesus Christ—at the center of your life. And not just your thinking life, but your doing and experiencing life. So it is good theology and good practice combined. If you get the cross right, then everything else works."

Paul Miller, Director of SeeJesus (www.seeJesus.net); author of *A Praying Life*

"I've dated a lot of different curriculum in the past, but there's very little worth taking home to meet Mom. Too often, the writing is too high (too theoretical—have you actually met a sinner before?), too emotive (talk to my head and my heart!), or too clunky (really? can I accomplish this in a week—much less an evening?). WHM's new Gospel Series small group materials are rifle-ready for the foot soldier in the church to use without a lot of training, and they seem to have been written by real sinners/strugglers for fellow sinners/strugglers. Thanks, WHM, for something I can actually use!"

Geoff Bradford, Pastor, Christ the King Presbyterian Church, Raleigh, NC

GOSPEL IDENTITY

GOSPEL IDENTITY

DISCOVERING WHO YOU REALLY ARE

Book One in the
Gospel Transformation Series

Serge

www.newgrowthpress.com

Gospel Identity: Discovering Who You Really Are
New Growth Press, Greensboro, NC 27404
www.newgrowthpress.com
Copyright © 2012 by World Harvest Mission.

All Scripture quotations, unless otherwise stated, are from the Holy Bible: New International Version®. (NIV®). Copyright ©1973, 1978, 1984 by International Bible Society. Used by permission of Zondervan. All rights reserved.

Gospel Identity: Discovering Who You Really Are is based on portions of discipleship material developed at World Harvest Mission by Paul E. Miller which was used as the basis for *Gospel Transformation* (copyright © 2001 by World Harvest Mission) written by Neil H. Williams.

Typesetting: Lisa Parnell, lparnell.com
Cover Design: Faceoutbooks, faceoutbooks.com

ISBN 978-1-936768-72-1

Printed in the United States of America

23 22 21 20 19 18 17 16   7 8 9 10 11

CONTENTS

INTRODUCTION

Welcome to *Gospel Identity: Discovering Who You Really Are!* This study is designed to help you discover who you already are in Jesus and how to live your new identity in your life, relationships, and ministry.

Gospel Identity, the first book in the "Gospel Transformation" series, focuses on the transformation of Christians by the power of the gospel. Before we get to that good news, we introduce this study by looking at the bad news that we are a fallen people who continue to justify ourselves apart from Jesus—which only serves to illustrate how thoroughly we *do* need Jesus. From there we'll examine the blessings we've been given through our new identity and new life in Jesus—justification, adoption, unity with Christ—how that helps us overcome our self-centeredness and idolatry, and how it pushes us outward so others can see and experience that new life in Jesus.

As you work through *Gospel Identity* as well as the other two books in the "Gospel Transformation" series—*Gospel Growth: Becoming a Faith-Filled Person* and *Gospel Love: Grace, Relationships, and Everything That Gets in the Way*—you'll be encouraged to lead a life of greater faith, repentance, and love.

How does "gospel transformation" occur? How does it relate to life? What *are* the essentials of the Christian life, and how do they change us? That's what this series is all about. Let's summarize it in four foundational points that we'll return to again and again.

1. Cheer up! The gospel is far greater than you can imagine! The gospel of Jesus Christ—and his power to transform our lives and relationships, communities, and ultimately, the nations—is the best news we will ever hear. It gives us a new identity not based on race, social class, gender, theology, or a system of rules and regulations, but on faith in Jesus—and it's an identity that defines every aspect of our lives. Because of this, we no longer have to hide from our sin and pretend that we have it all together. We now have a new way to live and relate to God and others every day. The good news is not only relevant to us when we first believe, but it continues to work in us and through us as we continue to believe and visibly expresses itself in love (Galatians 5:6).

2. Cheer up! You are worse than you think! One of the great hindrances to Christian growth, healthy relationships, and strong communities is a life of pretense. We pretend that we don't struggle with self-righteous attitudes, foul tempers, nagging anxieties, lustful looks, controlling and critical hearts, or a multitude of sins. We generally believe that we are better than other people. Part of the good news is that God knows all this—knows *us*—already, and he wants to be the one who changes us. Because our sin blocks our intimacy with God and others, we need God's Spirit to show us our many fears and offensive ways, and we need the insights of others to encourage us and speak into our lives.

Our first two points work together in a cyclical fashion. On the one hand, none of us wants to look at our sin without knowing the good news of forgiveness and deliverance from it. On the other hand, our view of the gospel is severely limited if we do not continually see the depths of our sin. The gospel cannot soak deeply into us unless it addresses our ongoing need for it. And that brings us to the third point.

3. Cheer up! God's Spirit works in your weakness! We not only have a new identity, but we have been given the Spirit who is more than sufficient to lead, guide, and empower us in our new life. The power that raised Jesus from the dead is at work in our new lives as well (Ephesians 1:19–20). Nevertheless, the power of the Spirit does not work automatically, but through repentant, obedient faith. Furthermore, this power is made evident through our weakness (2 Corinthians 12:9; 13:4). Along with Paul, we can delight in our weakness, for then we are strong, and God is glorified. The result is a wonderful freedom to forget about ourselves and stop wondering whether we have enough ability—we don't. But we can rejoice in the knowledge that God uses and empowers the weak. Therefore we have the hope discussed in point four.

4. Cheer up! God's kingdom is more wonderful than you can imagine!
The kingdom of God is the new and final age that began with Jesus' coming. It is the age of righteousness, peace, and joy in the Holy Spirit (Romans 14:17). The kingdom of God is about the renewing of all things, and God has made us a part of this great story of salvation. This kingdom is about the reconciliation of relationships, about the restoration of justice and equality, about freedom from every lord except Jesus, about forgiveness, and about the defeat of Satan. It is about compassion for the poor and powerless, about helping those who are marginalized and rejected by society, and about using our gifts and resources for the advancement of others. It is about new communities and the transformation of society and culture. For Paul, to preach the gospel is to preach the kingdom, and therefore to preach the whole counsel of God (Acts 20:24–27).

The goal of each study, therefore, is not simply to master the content, but to allow the gospel to master you and your group more fully. Knowledge is like bread—unless it is digested, it will go stale. The content of this course needs to be chewed, digested, and assimilated, so that true *spiritual* growth can occur. It's easy to slip into the routine of just completing the lesson, but don't. Our ultimate goal here is love—love rooted in a growing faith in Jesus, which leads to more love (Galatians 5:6).

Our prayer is that through your time together your love for Jesus—and the people God brings into your life—will grow deeper daily. May God bless and encourage your group as you work together through this study!

ABOUT THE SESSIONS

The sessions in this study are built to take 75 minutes apiece. They've been built so there's plenty of good content, but also plenty of room for discussion. There are suggested times for each section, but again do what you need to as a group—the goal isn't to master the content, but to allow the gospel to master you and your group.

Sessions follow a logical order, so be sure to cover them in the sequence given. Often, one session builds on what has been previously covered in the session or sessions before it. Furthermore, each session follows its own sequence so that your group can get the most impact from it. Each time you get together, you can expect to see the following:

Overview—This introduction of the session includes the one point to take away from the session. Reading it as part of your group time is optional, but by stating the focus up front everyone knows what's coming.

Opening the Discussion—In this brief opening section, take time to unwind and transition from your previous environment (home, work, or some other place) and into the theme of the session. The questions here are intended to help the entire group interact. They also help set up what comes later in the session. And maybe, because you were so busy having a good time discussing a "light" question, you won't even realize you've *already* gotten down to business.

Opening the Word—This is the heart of each session, and typically the longest section. You'll spend some serious time digging into God's Word and discovering its meaning in ways you hadn't before. More importantly, you'll discover how the information you're studying applies to your life right now, and what God wants to do with it.

Opening Your Life—In this closing section you'll move from *under-standing how* the Bible applies to your life to actually *applying* it. At the end of each session you will break into smaller groups or pairs to share how you will apply today's lesson and commit to following up with each other during the week. This way everyone's involved, engaged, and committed to one another. The lesson will usually give some suggestions for its application, but if God's telling you to do something else, *go for it!*

In short, in each session you'll be challenged to share, to think, and to act. And as you do, gospel transformation will be more than just the title of a Bible study series. It will be a reality you live every day.

FOR LEADERS

We strongly suggest working through each session on your own first, prior to your group time. Your prep time shouldn't require more than one-half hour, but take as much time as you need. Your goal is the same your group's—to grow in faith, repentance, and obedience. As you review the material, honestly answer each question. Ask the Spirit to reveal your own heart, and be prepared to share what the Spirit reveals with the group, as long as it's appropriate. Your own transparency and vulnerability will open the door for others.

You'll notice that there are times during the session (especially during "Opening Your Life") when we suggest getting into pairs or smaller groups. Feel free to do this at other times during the session when we haven't explicitly told you to do so. It's a great way to make sure everyone remains engaged with the material and with each other, and it frees people to share about matters they may not want to discuss with the entire group.

Also, in the back of the book are suggested answers and reflections relating to each session's questions. Don't use this section as a crutch or a shortcut. Wrestle with each question and passage on your own and as a group. Figure out its meaning for yourselves. Then, if you like, look in back to add further insight to your discussion time.

Finally, here are some expectations we encourage you to have for your group members, and to share openly with them:

1. **Expect to be challenged.** The answers will not come quickly or easily. If they do, we haven't done our job properly. As you work through each question, expect that it will take some time, thought, and soul-searching to complete each session.

2. **Expect the Holy Spirit** to be the one ultimately responsible for the growth of your group, and for the change in each person's life—including your own. Relax and trust him.

3. **Expect your group time together** to include an open, give-and-take discussion of each session's content and questions. Also expect times of prayer at each meeting. In fact, plan for them.

4. **Expect struggle.** Don't be surprised to find in your group a mixture of enthusiasm, hope, and honesty along with indifference, anxiety, skepticism, and covering up. We are all people who need Jesus every day, so expect your group to be made up of people who wrestle with sin and have problems—just like you!

5. **Expect to be a leader** who desires to serve, but who needs Jesus as much as the rest of the group. No leader should be put on a pedestal or be expected to have the right answers. Give yourself the freedom to share openly about your own weaknesses, struggles, and sins. Covet your group's prayers.

6. **Expect confidentiality**, and be prepared to ask the group to make that commitment with you. Anything personal must be kept in confidence and never shared with others outside the group. Gossip will quickly destroy a group.

You are ready to begin. May God bless your group's journey together!

FIRST, THE BAD NEWS . . .

OVERVIEW

In this session we'll explore how sin has broken us and the world we live in. Our struggles with identity start with our struggles with sin.

In this broken world, we will not—*cannot*—embrace the beauty and glory of the good news of Jesus Christ until we understand our own deep need and our sin. We are much like the rich young ruler (Matthew 19:16–22); we try to justify ourselves to Jesus and make our identity about what we *do*—until Jesus confronts us with that one area that clearly exposes us for what we *are*.

Therefore, we'll also look closely at our well-developed capacity for self-justification. We may not struggle with drugs or cheating the IRS, but we all justify ourselves as easily and automatically as we breathe. And until we face our sin rather than evade it, we will not give Jesus the room he needs to work in our lives. We cannot fully accept our new identity in Christ until we realize how deep our old identity goes.

Even as Christians, when we forget that we are sinners, we forget the gospel, and thus we short-circuit our ability to share it with the world around us that so desperately needs it. So as we confront the sin that pervades this world, let the battle begin within us.

OPENING THE DISCUSSION

Get into groups of three or four. Encourage people to get with others they'd like to know better, rather than those they already know well. Then, give groups five minutes to do the following:

1. Take a minute each to introduce yourselves to your group. There's one catch: you can't talk about what you *do*. No mention of jobs, hobbies, volunteer work—any kind of accomplishment or activity. So good luck—and *go*!

Allow up to five minutes, and then gather everyone back together. If this is your first time together as a group, ask *everyone* to introduce themselves and to take a few moments to share what they're hoping to get out of this study. Then discuss the following question:

2. Think about our opening activity. How does telling people what you do help them understand who you really are? How doesn't it help?

Leaders: The sections in *italics* are for you, to help you and your group transition from one part of the session to the next. Read them verbatim, put what's here in your own words, or just move on to the next section—whatever works best for you and your group.

---

*When did our identity become so wrapped up in **our** accomplishments, **our** actions, **our** words? When did what we do and what we say become more important to us, and to others, than who we are in Christ? The answer extends much further back in time than you might think.*

*Since the Garden of Eden, history has been marked by all people insisting on their way over God's—by justifying themselves apart from God. And our lives are lived out in the results of that rebellion every day. We all are broken people living in a broken world. Not **above** it—living **in** it. We need a savior and a new identity in Christ as desperately as the people around us. So let's start our time together by first exploring our broken world.*

OPENING THE WORD

> **50**
> MINUTES

Read Romans 8:18–22, then discuss these questions:

3. What evidence of "suffering" and "frustration" do you see around you? Come up with personal examples as well as "global" ones.

21

... bondage to decay ...

4. How do you normally respond to suffering or frustration? Confront, ignore, run the other way, complain but do nothing, something else? Explain.

— anything else is dust in the wind

Life's suffering and pressures can come from any direction, good or bad—family, friends, work, possessions, our health, our flesh, from Satan and the world—and can come at any time.

Have volunteers read 1 Kings 10:23–27; 11:1–4. Then discuss the following:

5. How do Solomon's blessings open the door for his sin?

> 24 wisdom God had put in his heart — brought fame + his wives 11:4 turned his heart after gods

6. What do you think your life would be like if you could go anywhere, or do or buy anything? Do you think you could handle both the blessings and the responsibility that comes with them? Explain.

> mideast peace, then notchwa then ... yes if its His plan ☺

Sometimes even the good things in our lives lead to suffering. When they do, it reveals something we don't like to hear—that the problem isn't only because of outside sin or influences, however much we're truly damaged by them. The problem is also us. And sometimes we'll do and say just about anything to avoid that truth.

Read Luke 10:25–29 and Revelation 3:1–3, and then discuss the following questions:

cont

7. What does it <u>mean to justify yourself</u>, based on these passages and your own experience? Why do we do it?

cont do it so cant justify myself

8. What are the consequences of justifying ourselves rather than leaving it to God—for ourselves and others around us?

see above

9. Look at the list in the table titled, "Excuses: How to be right and look good." Which of these excuses do you find yourself using to justify your actions? What are you really saying about yourself, and others, when you make these excuses?

Figure 1.1

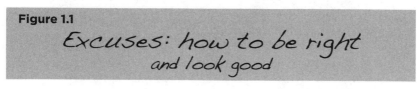

Excuses: how to be right and look good

- ▶ "I'm just weak."
  (It's not really my fault.)

- ▶ "I was just being honest."
  (Can't you handle the truth?)

- ▶ "I didn't mean to do it."
  (I didn't mean to get caught.)

- ▶ "It made me so angry."
  (I've been treated unfairly.)

- ▶ "I misunderstood you."
  (You're not as crazy as I thought!)

- ▶ "I'm just saying what I feel."
  (There's nothing wrong with my feelings.)

- ▶ "My family was like that."
  (You think I'm bad, you should meet my . . . .)

- ▶ "I'm having a bad day/week."
  (I deserve better.)

- ▶ "I'm tired . . . it's hot today!"
  (I deserve a break.)

- ▶ "I'm sorry, but you . . . ."
  (It's really your fault.)

- ▶ "I make mistakes."
  (Don't we all?)

- ▶ "I was only kidding."
  (Didn't you get the joke?)

- ▶ "You misunderstood me."
  (I'm not as bad as that.)

- ▶ "Nobody is perfect."
  (including you.)

- ▶ "That's just who I am."
  (I'm a sinner, you'll just have to live with that fact.)

- ▶ "I'm sorry, please forgive me."
  (Let's get this over with as quickly as possible.)

- ▶ "I'm just upset."
  (Can't you see that? The problem is that you're not compassionate.)

- ▶ "We have a personality problem."
  (You're half the problem.)

- ▶ "We have a communication problem."
  (You're half the problem.)

- ▶ "You're just too sensitive."
  (It's not my fault.)

Ask for volunteers to read Luke 6:37–45 and 1 John 1:8–10, and then discuss the following question:

10. What are we really saying when we claim we're not sinners or that someone else's sin is worse than ours?

he dont

"When Christ calls a man,
he bids him come and die."
—Dietrich Bonhoeffer

OPENING YOUR LIFE

Take turns reading together Psalm 73:1–28. Then discuss the following questions:

11. What is Asaph struggling with at the beginning of this psalm—both in terms of the world around him and within himself? What changes his perspective?

is my jealousy realize that you will take me into glory...

12. What area in your life do you most need to stop justifying yourself and your old identity—whether through words or actions—and replace your perspective with God's?

> *That I am imperfect and a sinner and so sin*

Get into smaller groups of three or four.

Think again about your answer to question 12. We don't want to just iden-tify the places we need to let God work in our lives; we also need to give God the opportunity to work.

*That's why, each week, you'll get the opportunity to respond to what God wants to do in your life. Below you'll find a few options, to help you think through how to put what you've learned in today's session into practice. Use any one of them—or if God has prompted you to do something else through this session, by all means do **that**!*

*In the space below, write down the one thing you'll do this week to apply today's lesson to your own life. Take ten minutes to share your choices with your group, and then make plans to check in with each other before the next session and encourage one another. Your touch-base time can be face-to-face, by phone, or online, but make a commitment you can keep—and then **keep** it.*

- Begin making a practice of holding your tongue when you want to defend yourself. Watch what happens when God defends you instead.

- Spend a few minutes at the end of each day reviewing your speech. When did you justify yourself instead of allowing God to? Confess this to God and ask his help in catching yourself before that next string of self-justification comes out.

- Who's dealing with bad news this week that you can lift up with your words? Make time for that person this week. The more time you spend lifting up others (and God), the less time you'll have for yourself. And you'll feel better, too.

This week I'll take on God's perspective by: _____

_____

_____

_____

After ten minutes close the session in prayer. Thank God for the relationships that are already beginning and growing in your group. Ask the Spirit to begin revealing areas of your lives that you're hiding from each other—and trying to hide from God. Ask for God's help in addressing those areas, as well as in those areas where the bad news of life is especially difficult for some group members right now.

ADDITIONAL NOTES:

. . . AND NOW, THE GOOD NEWS

2

OVERVIEW

In this session you'll gain a deeper understanding of the good news of Jesus Christ and why it's your good news too.

Have you ever noticed how everyone perks up when someone begins to tell a story? People who were lost in a sermon, class, or Bible study suddenly find their way again and see things afresh. Whether we are young or old, stories grab our attention. They often have a life-defining quality—in fact, it can be argued that we use them to make sense of our lives and world. Each culture and society has its own defining stories— the legends and history that reveal and reinforce the basis of that group's identity—for good *or* evil.

Families and individuals also have their own defining stories, each with their own characters, plot, conflicts, love and betrayal, tragedy, and hope. We love recalling our shared experiences because they've helped define and illustrate our relationships. They define how we think, how we be-have, and how we feel about others and about ourselves. However, our stories are by no means static. Sometimes they undergo significant revi-sions. Sometimes we take them *too* far—we have a fantasy world filled with stories where we are more successful; better known; more loved, admired, and desired; more in control; in better health; and living in peace and comfort. More pointedly, we like to make up stories to bring meaning and hope to our lives.

Thus, viewed in this light, and considering the gospel as a story, our lives are a conflict of stories—one trying to rule the other. Which story is real? Which one brings life and meaning? That's what we'll explore in this session.

OPENING THE DISCUSSION

1. What's your favorite story? How has that story affected and/or reflected your own life?

the Gospel

In our last session, we investigated the bad news—both in the world and in our own lives. Today we begin to look at the good news. First, let's take one more look at how we got here. Let's examine the biblical account of God's original good news—creation. Then we'll look at what went wrong and see how God addressed it by giving us the best news of all.

OPENING THE WORD

Read together through Genesis 1. Then discuss:

2. What are the most important themes in t*new* his chapter?

God created + it was good
" mom (kind) male + female
gave all to them

Have a volunteer read Genesis 3:1–12. Then discuss the following questions together:

3. Why do you think Adam and Eve ate the fruit? What do you suspect they were thinking and feeling at the time?

[handwritten notes]

4. What are some results of Adam and Eve's disobedience? How are they *already* different than they had been?

[handwritten notes]

5. Describe an experience in your own life when *you* were deliberately disobedient. Why did you do what you did? How did your deed affect you and others around you?

[handwritten notes]

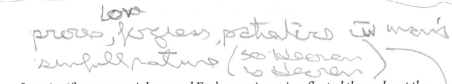

[handwritten notes]

In a significant way, Adam and Eve's experience is reflected throughout the Old Testament and the history of the nation God created, Israel. God gave his promises; God blessed his people; and yet his people rebelled. Repeatedly. They were incapable of obeying God's law; their hearts were hopelessly apart from God. Enter Jesus, the Son of God.

Read the following passages, and then discuss the questions that follow:

1 • Isaiah 9:6–7

2 • Luke 2:8–11

3 • Luke 4:16–21

4 • Acts 2:36–38

5 • Acts 5:42

6 • 1 Corinthians 15:1–4, 14–22

6. What is the "good news" according to these passages?

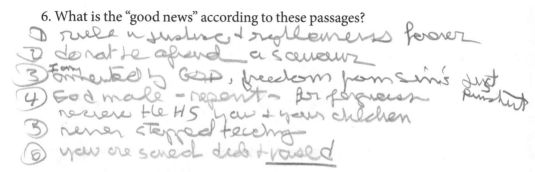

① rule n justice + righteousness forever
② do not be afraid — a saviour
③ anointed by God, freedom from sins just Punishnt
④ God made — repent — for forgiveness receive the HS you + your children
⑤ never stopped teaching
⑥ you are saved died + raised

7. What does this good news mean to you personally?

hope faith grace

8. What are the implications of the good news for you? For the people around you? For the world? In other words, what ought to change *because* of this good news? Give specific examples.

– not zero-sum now
– love your neybor
– core + shore
– not kill

> *"The greatest temptation that assails Christians is that in effect, for most of us, the Gospel has ceased to be news. And if it is not news it is not Gospel: for the Gospel is the proclamation of something absolutely new . . . . Any word that comes from God is news!"*
> —Thomas Merton,
> *Conjectures of a Guilty Bystander*

OPENING YOUR LIFE

20 MINUTES

The New Testament is the culmination of God's story so far and a call to the church to live its existence out of the "good news" story. As a community and as individuals, God calls us to continually connect to this great story and to live out of our new identity in Christ. But how do we do this? Where do we begin?

9. Think again about your answers to questions 7 and 8: how can you share *your* experience of the good news of Jesus in a way that your world can see and hear it? Share your ideas together as a group.

Get into pairs—if you have an odd number, a trio is okay.

How does what you've learned today apply to where you're at right now? How can you put it into practice? Choose from one of the options below—or if God has prompted you to do something else, do **that!** *In the space that follows write down the one thing you'll do this week to make today's session* *more real in your own life. Share your choices with your partner(s) and plan to check in with each other before the next session to encourage one another.*

- Who needs to hear the good news this week? Share it with that person. But don't just "share the gospel"—share how the good news of Jesus has changed *you* and how it can change your listener too.

- Who needs to *see* the good news this week? Serve that person as Jesus would. Don't even bring Jesus into it unless they ask. But be ready to share if they do.

- How have you let the good news become "yesterday's news"? Talk to God about it. Ask him to reconnect you to his great story and to provide opportunities for you to experience and express it.

This week, I'll respond to the good news of Jesus by: _____

_____

_____

_____

After ten minutes, get back together and close in prayer.

Thank God for the good news of Jesus Christ. Ask for the Spirit's help in guiding each group member into opportunities where they can share and live out the good news before others.

GOD MAKES IT RIGHT

OVERVIEW

In this session you'll discover the meaning of justification by faith—in God's eyes and in your everyday lives.

God is making the whole world right, and part of this work is making and declaring *us* right. Through Jesus, God gives us a new reputation, a new status, and a new image. Jesus has taken away our shame. He has reconciled us to himself and removed the power, bondage, and guilt of sin.

Paul writes in Romans 8:1, "Therefore, there is now no condemnation for those who are in Christ Jesus." Part of the ongoing struggle in the Christian life is not only continually believing these truths, but living as if we did. We agree that we are justified by faith; however, we often struggle to connect this to our daily lives—as we relate to our family, as we speak to others, or as we go about our work.

In this session we will not only explore what justification by faith means, but also introduce some practical ways we can apply it. We'll begin this process today by returning to our problem of self-justification—the use of our tongues and our desire to be right and look good—and then seek to bring the doctrine of justification by faith into those areas.

OPENING THE DISCUSSION

1. Describe a time you did something you thought was pretty great, but no one noticed or cared. How did you feel?

— "neat" who's measure?
'purs or
Gods

— net works

why is beloved if true, but works is love?

2. Why is so hard to do something good without having it acknowledged? After all, noticed or not, it's *something good.*

So far, we've explored both the bad news and the good news and how we continue to deal with both. Adam started an avalanche—a seemingly small sin that grew into an avalanche of sin, condemnation, and death for the entire human race. However, Jesus started an even greater avalanche of grace, righteousness, and life. love

*In this session we begin holding both sides in tension—looking at both our almost constant penchant for self-justification **and** the grace and justification offered by Jesus. Let's begin by looking at the aftermath of Adam and Eve's sin—specifically how it affected **their** children.*

OPENING THE WORD

Together read Genesis 4:3–16. Then discuss the following question:

3. Outwardly it appears as though both Cain and Abel do the right thing. Why do you think God approves of Abel's offering and not Cain's?

4. In what ways does Cain justify himself throughout this passage?

5. We may not react as strongly as Cain, but how *do* we react to people who reveal our self-justification for what it is—whether they do it intentionally, or like Abel, unintentionally?

Take turns reading Romans 4:1–8 and Romans 5:12–21. Then, discuss
the following questions:

R5 : 3→5

6. What are some of the blessings that are now yours because of Jesus,
according to these passages?

- justifies
- forgiveness of transgressions, sins covered
- redeems sins
- cross always justifies lessens sin 5/20

7. How would you describe what justification by faith is, based on these
and other passages you're aware of?

Romans 10 : 17 → ministry
4 : 16 +
Gal 3 : 2-14 faith rat needs
Gal 5 : 5 faith → hope

Grace p9 -1st
Isaiah 44 : 21-23
Job 14 : 17
33 : 26

8. How should this incredible gift from God remove our need to justify
ourselves? Give specific examples.

Eph 2 : 8

= works

hope ...

*One of the greatest struggles of the Christian life is the struggle over righ-
teousness, reputation, and glory. The battle is over whether we will choose
to live out of our new identity and the gospel's verdict of us as "righteous,"
or whether we will try to build our own reputations instead—and maybe
even try to use the gospel to justify **that**.*

"The world runs by ungrace. Everything depends on what I do . . . . Jesus' kingdom calls us to another way, one that depends not on our performance but his own. We do not have to achieve but merely follow. He has already earned for us the costly victory of God's acceptance."
—Philip Yancey, What's So Amazing About Grace?

OPENING YOUR LIFE

We love to be right, we love to be strong; we hate to be weak, we hate to be wrong. We love the strength that comes from youth, money, beauty, intelligence, prestigious work, good health, or fame. We work hard to maintain these supposed positions of strength. We hate to take the weak position, the position of powerlessness. Likewise, as soon as we wake up every day, our hearts are seeking new ways to be justified. We long to think better of ourselves, and for others to think the same. We're quick to put others down in order to improve or preserve our own reputations.

*Nevertheless, as we place ourselves in the position of strength and "rightness," we separate ourselves from grace and from the Spirit's power in our lives. Jesus' power is "made perfect in weakness" (2 Corinthians 12:9). We also distance ourselves from other people, especially those close to us. I am right about how my home should be run. I am right about how the church should function. I am right about my enemies, and I know why they are so wrong. I study hard to be right about all sorts of things. What do you think it is like to **live** with me? You're right.*

Let's think back to the "great" accomplishments we shared about in question 1 and discuss them in more depth.

9. In the situation you thought of in question 1—or any others that come to mind—how did you attempt to add *to* your reputation by trying to appear better, smarter, wiser, funnier, or holier?

10. How have you tried adding to your reputation by subtracting from others' reputations, by belittling their accomplishments or contributions? In what ways?

Read Isaiah 53:1–12, and discuss the following questions:

11. What do Jesus' actions imply about our desire to justify ourselves?

12. What do Jesus' actions imply about how to respond when we see others justifying themselves?

It takes time for our hearts to be transformed so that our desire to understand and cling to God's justification rather than our own becomes our "default mode." We'll spend future sessions addressing this. But we can begin today by addressing what comes out of us—how we hurt others when we justify ourselves. (assessing)

Think about your answers today. What form of self-justification normally comes out of you first? Gossip, complaining, criticism, boasting, blameshifting, self-defense, lying? Instead of giving you options to choose from this week, let's work on addressing the thing you know you're struggling with.

Find a partner now—groups of three are okay. Share briefly about what you're dealing with right now, and then take a few minutes to pray for each other. Also, set a time to touch base before our next session, to encourage and pray for each other. In the space that follows, write down what you're doing in response to this week's session. When you're done praying, stay quiet or move into another room, to give other pairs a chance to share and pray together. May God grow each of you deeper in faith as you seek to rest in his justification and reputation rather than your own!

This week, I'll address my habit of self-justification by: _____

_____

_____

_____

ADDITIONAL NOTES:

JOIN THE FAMILY

OVERVIEW

In this session you'll understand our adoption into God's family and how to experience better relations with your fellow family members.

One of the most remarkable blessings of our salvation is our adoption into God's new family. We are now children of the living God, restored to an intimate and loving relationship with our creator. We now have all the rights, privileges, and status of God's sons and daughters. This is our new, and true, identity.

This session focuses on applying this wonderful truth to everyday life and on uncovering areas where we're not trusting in our Father's ongoing love, protection, care, direction, and discipline. Adoption is about an intimate relationship with our heavenly Father; therefore, it speaks directly to our anxieties, fears, worries, and lack of love for others. Adoption also connects us directly to each other—we are all one family—and so it has implications for how we view and treat other Christians.

As we consider our adoption into God's family, we need to acknowledge that the way we view our relationship with our earthly fathers shapes and colors the way we view our heavenly Father. And that's where our discussion begins today.

OPENING THE DISCUSSION

1. What was your relationship with your father like growing up? If you did not have a father, substitute your mother or guardian.

good, lonely and overly smothered
— caretaking —

2. What are some pleasant memories of your father? What were some ways your father disappointed or harmed you?

1 kitchen   *— divorce*
+ trips

3. In what ways do you think your relationship with your earthly father has affected the way you view your heavenly Father?

only good

Our earthly fathers provide a picture of fatherhood by the way they treated us—their love or abuse, their smiles or frowns, their encouraging or biting words, their praise or condemnation, their attention or neglect, their laughter or anger, their generosity or selfishness. A good father provides a picture of what God is like. However, even an absent or abusive father can fuel the imagination for what an involved, caring father would be like and prepare our hearts to desire a deeper relationship with our heavenly Father.

OPENING THE WORD

40
MINUTES

Divide into six subgroups (a "group" of one is okay). Take ten minutes to read one of the passages from the list below and discuss questions 4 and 5.

Leader: If your group has fewer than six people, get into three subgroups (a group of one is okay), each taking two passages.

- Acts 2:21
  w Moner calls on God
- Romans 8:14–17
  if lead by Gods spirit
- Romans 8:38–39
  not separateable

- Galatians 3:23–27
  law →tutor→ faith
  guardian
- Galatians 4:1–7
  no longer but son)
- Hebrews 2:10–15
  though JC

4. What does it mean to be a child of God, according to your passage(s)?

5. What <u>encourages</u> you about this passage? What intimidates you? Which ideas here do you have trouble fully understanding?

all   *none*

Come back together after ten minutes and share highlights and insights from your discussion time. Continue your discussion together.

6. Think about the things that worry or <u>frighten you</u>. When faced with those things, what do you tend to turn to for comfort or security other than your heavenly Father?

health — DR
$ — wife

7. How do your anxieties expose what you are putting your faith in? When we doubt God's love for us as his sons and daughters, we can de-velop the mindset of being a spiritual orphan (see John 14:18). In what ways do you respond like an orphan, rather than as a child of God?

↳ visits (family / friends)
↳ then go home

"If you want to judge how well someone understands Christianity, find out how much he makes of the thought of being God's child, and having God as his Father."
—J. I. Packer

6 →

Read 1 Peter 5:7–11, and then discuss the following:

8. What are some healthy ways we can respond to our anxieties?

proportion: suffer for a little while (while on earth)

9. How might understanding and believing that you *really* have been adopted into God's family change the way you see yourself? The way you see others?

understand how we act
live to love → anger →
→ selfhood →
→ blame

OPENING YOUR LIFE

20
MINUTES

Read together 1 John 3:10–18, and then discuss the following:

10. What are the implications of this passage when it comes to our relationship with others, especially other Christians?

(handwritten) — JC is begotten, the one adopted
— love one another (11)
in deed + truth (18)
(act) + (carry out)

11. Reread verse 16. What would laying down your life for others, just as God's Son did for you, look like right now? Give specific examples.

(handwritten) — donate time to listen + teach
(time is given) + invite to your
— passions can be accumulated and passed on
— in crisis fall on the episode
— don't pursue an argument or hurt

Get into groups of three or four.

*How does what you've learned today apply to where you're at right now? How can you put it into practice? Choose from one of the options below—or if God has prompted you to do something else, do **that**! In the area below, write down the one thing you'll do this week to make today's session more real in your own life. Share your commitment with your partners and plan to connect with each other before the next session to check in and encourage one another.*

- Think about your answer to question 10 again. What one concrete step can you take this week to not only have an answer, but *be* an answer in someone else's life? Take that step this week.

- Do you still struggle with the idea that you are God's child? Spend some time talking with your heavenly Father about it. Ask God to help you truly receive that truth into your life, and to begin living out of that truth.

- What's one way you can build up your relationships with God's family? Invite someone from church over for dinner, or sit down for coffee with him or her. You might even try this with the people you're with now.

This week, I'll respond out of my sonship to God by: _____

_____

_____

_____

After ten minutes, get back together and close in prayer.

Thank your heavenly Father for who he is, and for his mercy in welcoming you into his family. Pray that group members would live out that spirit of sonship both in their personal lives and in their relationships with others.

ADDITIONAL NOTES:

A NEW LIFE IN CHRIST

OVERVIEW

In this session you'll develop a deeper understanding of your union with Jesus and how to live out of your "in-Christ"-ness.

Pretend for a moment that you're an advanced student of music, looking at a beautiful, complex piece of classical music. You might have the ability to examine the piece quite thoroughly. You could analyze its melody, harmony, and rhythm. However, you will never be struck by its beauty, majesty, and poetry until you hear it performed by a master pianist—or better yet, until you have learned and performed it yourself.

Likewise, our new life in Christ is not only something believed but also something lived, something seen, something experienced. It is determined by who Christ is and what he has done, and it is something we continue to learn tangibly as we follow and obey Jesus. Paul frequently uses the phrase "in Christ" (about one hundred times). It is virtually synonymous with being a Christian. A man or woman who is in Christ is a Christian. This lesson concentrates on this central truth of the gospel and explores some practical applications.

OPENING THE DISCUSSION

1. Share about something you were really "into" for a while—something you were incredibly excited about doing. How did that thing or activity also, in a sense, get into you? In other words, how did it affect other things in your life?

2. When did that thing or activity stop exciting you? Why?

*Today we're going to explore the ultimate "into"—our new lives in Christ. So far in this study we've explored numerous benefits of the Christian life, including forgiveness, justification, adoption, and sonship. But as incredible as these benefits are, the Christian life is more than any of those things, or even their sum total. Above all else, the Christian life is life **in Christ**. It is union, and communion, with Christ.*

And that fact changes everything—or should. Our life in Christ is not a one-time thing we should get tired of, but a literally never-ending adventure. So let's explore what it means to be "in Christ," and how we can better live it.

OPENING THE WORD

50 MINUTES

Take turns reading Romans 6:1–11; Romans 8:35–39; Romans 12:4–5; and Ephesians 2:8–10. Then discuss the following questions:

3. According to these passages, what does it mean to be in Christ?

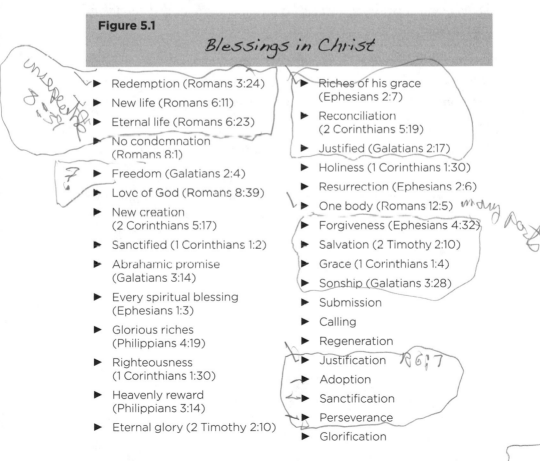

Figure 5.1

Blessings in Christ

- Redemption (Romans 3:24)
- New life (Romans 6:11)
- Eternal life (Romans 6:23)
- No condemnation (Romans 8:1)
- Freedom (Galatians 2:4)
- Love of God (Romans 8:39)
- New creation (2 Corinthians 5:17)
- Sanctified (1 Corinthians 1:2)
- Abrahamic promise (Galatians 3:14)
- Every spiritual blessing (Ephesians 1:3)
- Glorious riches (Philippians 4:19)
- Righteousness (1 Corinthians 1:30)
- Heavenly reward (Philippians 3:14)
- Eternal glory (2 Timothy 2:10)

- Riches of his grace (Ephesians 2:7)
- Reconciliation (2 Corinthians 5:19)
- Justified (Galatians 2:17)
- Holiness (1 Corinthians 1:30)
- Resurrection (Ephesians 2:6)
- One body (Romans 12:5)
- Forgiveness (Ephesians 4:32)
- Salvation (2 Timothy 2:10)
- Grace (1 Corinthians 1:4)
- Sonship (Galatians 3:28)
- Submission
- Calling
- Regeneration
- Justification
- Adoption
- Sanctification
- Perseverance
- Glorification

4. What does being in Christ mean to you personally? Why is your life different because of that truth? Put it in your own words.

Understanding our union with Christ helps us to understand the blessings we already have in Christ. And understanding those blessings—really understanding them—frees us to live the kind of lives God created us to live. So today we're discussing what God is trying to teach us, and also taking time to reflect on who we really are in Christ. Start now.

Take two or three minutes to quietly read through and reflect upon the list of "Blessings in Christ." Don't just glance through the list. Take at least a few moments to try to grasp the meaning of each blessing before moving on to the next one.

After two to three minutes, regain everyone's attention. Then discuss the following questions:

5. Which of these blessings is the most meaningful to you right now? And what, specifically, does it mean to you?

6. Which blessings do you find difficult to understand or accept? Why?

freedom

Take time to wrestle with question 6 as a group before moving on. If someone really needs help receiving a particular blessing that *belongs* to him or her in Christ—and they *all* do—try working through it together. Understanding might not come right away, but at least give it the opportunity to come.

7. Does the fact that we have a hard time understanding or feeling that we really have these blessings change the fact that we *do*? How would you advise someone else to stay in these truths even when he or she's not "feeling" them?

The benefits of the gospel are ours in full! Nothing can separate us from the love of God (Romans 8:38–39). We are sons and daughters who are dearly loved, rejoiced over, and delighted in. That is who we really are—defined by who we are in Christ, not by our sin.

Paul didn't begin his letters to the churches "To all those at Rome with whom God is angry," or "To the church at Corinth, which continually tests God's patience," or "To all the rebels at Philippi," rather, he says, "Grace and peace, dearly loved, dear children, saints," and so on. You may not feel holy and pleasing, but so what? You are holy and pleasing because you are in Christ, and your works from faith are accepted. When a young child draws a picture for her father—even if it is very imperfect—the father loves it, sticks it on his refrigerator, and proudly shows it off to everyone. Likewise, what you do in faithful relationship to your heavenly Father is accepted and delightful to him.

"Love God and do what you want."
— St. Augustine

We are truly free in Christ. However, we often have not freed ourselves to live the way Jesus has called us. Take a minute to quietly review the chart on the next page, particularly the first two columns. Try to avoid reading the right two columns for now—just focus on the columns called "Acting like" and "You're in bondage to."

Then pick back up with the questions below.

8. Which of these mentalities do you most often fall victim to? What does it look like in your case?

Figure 5.2

Christian, have you forgotten who you really are?

Acting like:	You're in bondage to:	You've forgotten your:	What God says about you:
A slave?	people's "rules"— your own and others'	freedom in Christ	Galatians 4:6–9
An orphan?	fear: of rejection, failure, punishment	adoption in Christ	1 John 3:1–3
A Pharisee?	appearances, pretense, criticism	justification in Christ	Philippians 3:8–11
A POW?	a particular sin	sanctification in Christ	Romans 6:12–22
A hermit?	self-interest, individualism	union with others in Christ	Romans 12:4–10
Eeyore?	death	resurrection in Christ	Romans 6:3–11
Mr. Scrooge?	material possessions, the good life	inheritance in Christ	Ephesians 4:22–32
A tyrant?	manipulation, anger, power	submission to Christ	1 Peter 5:1–7

© 2006 World Harvest Mission

9. What usually causes the forgetting—both in terms of outside triggers and internal feelings or thoughts?

Now, take a couple more minutes to read the other columns. Take time also to look up the accompanying Bible passages; if we've already read a verse today, read it again now, in light the "old" mentality you struggle with. Then let's discuss together:

10. According to this chart in what ways do you forget, or not believe, that you're united to Christ? Rephrase that in your own words.

11. How did the Bible passages you just read address your particular "old" mentality? Explain.

Figure 5.3

The Christian life is lived out of our union with Christ. We:

- ► Speak in Christ (2 Corinthians 2:17)
- ► Do good works in Christ (Ephesians 2:10)
- ► Hope in Christ (1 Corinthians 15:19)
- ► Glory in Christ (Philippians 3:3)
- ► Work together in Christ (Romans 16:3)
- ► Marry in Christ (2 Corinthians 6:14)
- ► Live in Christ (Galatians 2:20)
- ► Die in Christ (1 Thessalonians 4:16)
- ► Love others in Christ (1 Corinthians 16:24)
- ► Suffer in Christ (Philemon 1:23)
- ► Have joy in Christ (Philippians 1:26)
- ► Give thanks in Christ (1 Thessalonians 5:18)
- ► Live a godly life in Christ (2 Timothy 3:12)

OPENING YOUR LIFE

15 MINUTES

Divide into subgroups of three or four.

*Now that we've addressed who we are in Christ—and even how we sometimes forget it—how do we **live** in Christ? What does that look like? Take the next fifteen minutes to explore that together in your groups.*

Instead of giving you options to choose from, there's one more chart—"The Christian life is lived out of our union with Christ"—for you to read and reflect on today. Again, don't just glance at this chart, but take at least a few moments to think about how each aspect of being in Christ pertains to your life before moving on to the next one.

Then, reflect on these questions: What is God calling you to do right now? What's one way you can respond to your world this week, out of your new life in Christ? Write down your response below.

When everyone is ready, discuss what God's shown you. And if you're still stuck on trying to receive your blessings in Christ, that's okay—share that. Allow God to deal with you wherever you are. Also, set up a time to touch base with each other, to continue encouraging and praying for one another, before the next session.

When you're done sharing, take time to pray for one another. I'll close our prayer time together after fifteen minutes.

This week I'll live out who I am in Christ by: _____

_____

_____

_____

After fifteen minutes close prayer time by reading Ephesians 3:14–21 as a blessing over your entire group.

SINNERS IN THE HANDS OF A LOVING GOD

6

OVERVIEW

In this session we'll learn to how to live out of the fact that God's wrath or anger is completely satisfied in Christ. We'll learn how to live in a way that's relational and not merely legal.

One of the barriers to faithful living is the repeated occurrence of our many sins. In the face of all our failures to do better, the gospel often seems too good to be true—and we seem too bad for God to truly love. Thus, a continuing struggle in our lives is to believe that we are God's children and in a right relationship with him.

Sadly, some people view the Christian life in a purely legal framework. They believe if you step outside the bounds, you are under God's wrath and condemnation. In such an environment, it is easy to slip into a mentality of thinking we have to do better and "shape up" to appease an angry God—or other angry Christians!

This lesson seeks to solidify the foundation of Christian living—the death and resurrection of Jesus, not our performance. Because of Jesus' death and resurrection we are sons and daughters who are loved and forgiven, not criminals awaiting punishment. We will come to view the Christian life relationally rather than legally, and be glad that God is always for us, with us, and in us.

OPENING THE DISCUSSION

Get into groups of three or four, and take five minutes to discuss the following:

1. When has someone—a parent, a boss, someone from your former church, or someone else— made you feel "not good enough"? How did you respond? Did you try harder, get angry, judge them in return, give up, or do something else? Explain.

Bring everyone back together after five minutes. Ask a volunteer from each group to share his or her answer.

Feeling not good enough is rough. But as bad as other people can make us feel, it's worse to feel we've failed God, or that he's just waiting for us to make a mistake so that he can punish us for it. Hopefully it has become clear during the first half of our study that God is both just and merciful, and that Jesus has already paid the price for our sins. Our entire new identity in Christ is based on this latter fact.

*Still, it's easy to slip back into the idea that we have to do everything just right to please God. As sinners, we will never be perfect. We will always have to confess and ask God's help to live the lives he's called us to. But the good news is that God **wants** us to bring everything to him—the good and the bad—so **he** can make us even better, so each of us can grow in his love. Truly believing that is what changes us.*

OPENING THE WORD

*"Yea, as your great trouble
is about the Father's love, so you can no way
more trouble or burden him, than by your
unkindness in not believing of it."*
— John Owen

Take turns reading through Luke 15:11–32. Then discuss the following questions:

2. What words would you use to describe the younger son when he left home, and when he returned? *young wild dead lost*

meek & repentant joyful loved alive found

3. What if the prodigal son had become prodigal again after this? At what point do you feel the father would just be "enabling" him?

4. How did the Father communicate his love to *both* sons? Come up with as many examples as you can. *Gave + celebrate*

— all yours + withme

5. When has someone believed in you long past the point where you deserved it? Share about that person and what he or she did. How were you affected by it?

Have volunteers read Romans 3:20–28; 5:6–10; and Ephesians 2:4–9. Then discuss the following questions:

6. What do these passages say about God's wrath and judgment of those who believe and place their trust in him? *cept your faith in Jesus*

slaves never grace

7. How *does* sin affect our relationship with God? Share examples from Scripture as well as from your own life, as much as you're willing.

[handwritten notes: "feel krus" with arrow; "testing, teaching"; "Is 59"]

8. Why do we usually stop going back to God after we repeatedly sin? Are we right to do so? Explain.

> If the issue of God's anger with sin is a particularly large one with you or your group, we've added a special section at the end of this session so you can go into more depth. See "Is God Always Angry with Me When I Sin?" on page 58.

If we think God's anger or pleasure with us is based totally on what we do, and not in terms of what Jesus has done on the cross, we're in trouble. Fortunately, as we discussed in our last session, we are in Christ and that's how God views us.

Still, the question remains: "What shall we say, then? Shall we go on sinning so that grace may increase?" (Romans 6:1). Clearly, continuing in willful sin is not living a life of faith. The life of faith says, "I really do want to live a life pleasing to God. Lord, show me how and help me to actually do it."

Our sin can still grieve the Spirit and we can come under our Father's discipline. However, this does not change our identity—who we are in Christ—and how we are to view other Christians. With this understanding, we can admit our sins and failures. And because we can be honest about our own shortcomings before God, we invite others to approach (or re-approach) God as well.

OPENING YOUR LIFE

Ask for a volunteer to read 1 John 4:11–19, and then discuss the following questions:

9. When has sharing how God has loved you opened a door for someone else to experience God's love? Talk about it.

— *m human reel flee term*
parable

— *fear punhut*

10. In what ways do you most need to be perfected in love right now?

Divide into smaller groups of three or four.

*How can you make God's love for you more visible to others this week? Choose from one of the options below—or if God has prompted you to do something else, do **that**! In the area below, write down the one thing you'll do this week to make today's session more real in your own life. Take five minutes to share your commitment with your partners and make plans to connect with each other before the next session to encourage one another.*

- Where do you still struggle with fearing punishment? Spend some time this week confessing it to God—and better yet, also to another Christian you trust. Your transparency might open up an avenue of healing for both of you.

- Who's a "prodigal" you need to love—someone who's either walked away from God or church? Spend some time with that person this week. Listen way more than talk—allow him or her to see Christ in you, rather than just *you*.

- Who doesn't know God's love and *needs* to know? Share your own experience of God's freedom from sin and fear with that person. Don't push for a response; give that person time to process what you've said. But be ready to follow up when he or she is ready.

This week, I'll respond to God's persistent love by: _____

_____

_____

_____

After five minutes, get back together and close in prayer.

Thank your heavenly Father for his perfect, boundless love. Ask God to drive out the fear that still resides in your life and to express his love through you in a way that the world around you can see and receive it.

Is God always angry with me when I sin?

We need to be careful how we answer this question, maintaining a relational view of Christianity rather than a purely legal framework. Unfortunately, some would answer our question above with an unqualified "yes." In a legal framework the emphasis is on external sins and obedience. With such an understanding, it's easy to *appear* obedient—there's less apparent sin for God to get angry about! A typical legal answer is, "When I disobey, I no longer live under God's blessing." A real-life example goes like this: "When I travel at 56 mph (one mile over the speed limit) I have moved outside of the sphere of God's love." But is this correct—especially when we ask a few follow-up questions about the extent of heart disobedience in our lives?

If God is always angry with you when you sin, consider the following questions:

- How often do you disobey God? Quite a bit? Well then, God must be angry with you fairly often. What about the many sins that you're not even aware of? What about ongoing sins, like lust and anger?
- How good is the best thing you've ever done? Luke 17:10 says, "So you also, when you have done everything you were told to do, should say, 'We are unworthy servants; we have only done our duty.'" If God only smiles when you are "good," it would be a very small, infrequent smile indeed. After all, who is good but God alone (Mark 10:18)? How much more "good" will you have to do before God will smile on you continually?
- James 2:10 says, "For whoever keeps the whole law and yet stumbles at just one point is guilty of breaking all of it." Hypothetically, if you broke only one of God's commands then, because of the interconnectedness of God's commands, for all intents and purposes you have broken them all.

If we see God's anger or pleasure in terms of what we do, and not in terms of what Christ has done on the cross, we find that God is not pleased at all. If God is always angry when we sin, either we end up believing that he is angry at us all the time, or we end up claiming that we are not that great of sinners!

Of course, this raises the question "Then may I sin so that grace may abound? Why shouldn't I go 100 mph because of the security of the gospel? Since God smiles on me, I can do what I want." Clearly, this is not a life of faith.

The life of faith says, This is such good news! I really do want to live a life pleasing to God; Lord, show me my offensive ways (Psalm 139:23–24). Faith says, You are pleasing to God; now go and be pleasing. You are righteous; now go and be righteous. You are loved; now go and be loving (1 John 4:11). You are forgiven; now go and be forgiving. The Christian life is to flow from faith in the good news, not from unbelief that considers God's anger or love dependent on my feeble performance. There is a huge difference between "God is pleased with me when I sin. Yes! I can do what I want," and "God is pleased with me even though I sin; so out of this good news I want to live a life pleasing to him."

My heavenly Father delights in me and rejoices over me (Zephaniah 3:17), and he disciplines me for my good (Hebrews 12:5–11). As his son or daughter I now have his Spirit dwelling in my heart (Galatians 4:6). His Spirit is the one who now fights against the sin in my life. Nevertheless, my relationship with him can still be disrupted through my sin. I can still grieve the Spirit by my sin (Ephesians 4:30). I can temporarily disrupt our relationship with sins like anger and gossip. In such cases I sadden the Spirit, but his sadness is for my good. It is really the Spirit's longing to work in my life, to change me, and to make me more like Jesus.

In conclusion, it may be helpful to make a distinction between three different questions in our discussion:

- Is God always angry with *me*? (an identity question)
- Does God delight in sin? (an ethical question)
- Does my sin affect my relationship with God? (a relationship question)

The identity question. God has dealt with my sin—past, present, and future. He has removed my sins as far as the east is from the west, and now I am a new creation. I am in Christ. This is my new identity. Everything that belongs to Jesus is mine. God does not delight in sin, but he does delight in me. Once I was an object of God's anger; now I am an object of his pleasure. I am holy, righteous, accepted, loved, forgiven, and delighted in. This is how I should view myself and other Christians. This is the good news that I need to live out of every day. With this understanding, I can admit my sins and failures because I know God is not angry with me.

The ethics question. God is holy, and takes no delight in evil. No sin is pleasing to God. I also should not delight in sin. I still need to repent of the flesh and its acts. I am still responsible for my sin, and cannot be neutral or ambivalent toward it. Moreover, anything I do that does not come from faith and repentance is unacceptable to God—hay, wood, and stubble—to be burned up on the last day.

The relationship question. We affect God by our lives and actions. God's emotional response to our sin is varied. He is not cold, remote, uninvolved, or emotionless. Jonah reminds us: God is gracious and compassionate, slow to anger and abounding in love (Jonah 4:2). My sin can still grieve the Spirit and I can come under my Father's discipline. However, this does not change who I am in Christ and how I am to view other Christians. With this understanding, I can admit my sins and failures because I know that sin brings distance to my relationship with God and grieves my Father.

YOU ARE WHAT YOU WORSHIP

OVERVIEW

In this session you'll become aware of the nature, power, and extent of idolatry in our lives.

This lesson introduces the theme of idolatry. It is designed to help us recognize unbelief in our hearts and how unbelief expresses itself in sinful behavior. Of course, there is no way to cover all the ways unbelief shows itself, but we can learn to think in categories that will enable us to recognize our sin, unbelief, and idolatry.

Often we think of idolatry as nothing more than making gods out of wood and stone. However, this is only one expression of idolatry. The New Testament also warns us against falling into idolatry. In 1 Corinthians 10:14, Paul urges the Corinthians to flee from idolatry. In Galatians 5:20, Paul lists idolatry as one of the acts of the flesh. And in Colossians 3:5, he writes, "Put to death, therefore, whatever belongs to your earthly nature: sexual immorality, impurity, lust, evil desires and greed, which is idolatry."

Sin is more than just what we do outwardly. Sin is a heart condition before it becomes a behavior. What we truly worship in our hearts reveals who we are and what we find our identity in. Thus, the idols we hold onto prevent us from fully embracing our new identity in Jesus and ultimately lead us into outward sin. Therefore, our idols need to be identified so that the gospel can be applied to them.

OPENING THE DISCUSSION

Leader: You're going to begin your group time a little differently today—with a time of worship. If a group member has a musical gift, let him or her use it and lead everyone in song for the first 5 to 10 minutes. Or, play a worship song softly enough that your group can sing over it. Use this time to lift up your voices and focus on God together. If opening with a worship time is something you normally do as a group, then go directly to question 1.

1. Why is it so important to worship God? Come up with as many ideas as you can.

— He knows, to we are remind ourself
by giving an love
— everything others

For all the reasons we've just come up with and more, God's "worthship" deserves to be recognized by us, always. It is only because God is worthy that we too have any worth—and a new identity in Christ. When we worship anything other than God, we devalue his creation—ourselves included.

Today, we're going to pinpoint the things we worship other than God, often unintentionally. We're also going to examine how those things pull us away from the worship God deserves, how idolatry undermines our new identity in Christ, and what we can do about it.

— Levels
— wealth

OPENING THE WORD

40 MINUTES

Take turns reading Exodus 20:3–6; 32:1–8; and 1 John 5:18–21. Then discuss the following questions:

2. Why does God consider idolatry a sin, according to these passages?

created idol not God so outside

5–18–21) "son")

3. In Exodus 32:1–8, how had the Israelites already turned away from God—committing idolatry in their hearts—even before they created a physical idol to worship?

Trusted a man moses who went missing —now turned to idols

An idol is anything apart from Jesus that we believe we need to make us happy, satisfied, or fulfilled. The reasons we resort to idolatry aren't hard to find. Whenever we feel a great lack, need, deficiency, or alienation, we look to fill that void. We serve, love, desire, trust, fear, and worship other things apart from God to give us love, joy, peace, freedom, status, identity, control, happiness, security, fulfillment, health, pleasure, significance, acceptance, and respect.

Sometimes our idols are obviously wrong. However, the things we desire are often good in themselves, such as having well-behaved children or taking pride in our work. If this becomes an *inordinate desire*, it has become a false god. Even *good things become idols* when they start to rule our lives.

We're going to take some time to identify the idols, or potential idols, in our own lives. Understanding our old "default modes" will help us catch ourselves and realize it's time to turn back to God and worship him instead.

Fears, trusts, and desires are all things that can rule our lives instead of Jesus—or can push us toward other idols. So that's where we'll start. Take a few minutes to work through the following list on your own. Check any items that you feel particularly relate to your life. We'll discuss them as a group afterward.

I fear . . .   (*lately kind highs*)

☐ People's rejection, attacks, or control

☐ Losing, or not gaining, a reputation

☐ My boss firing or getting angry at me

☐ My children turning out badly

☐ Exposure of sin, my past

☐ My spouse/friend rejecting me

☐ Losing an inheritance

☐ My spouse/friend telling on me

☐ Punishment

☐ Losing control

☒ Lack of money *plem for*

☐ Going crazy

☐ Middle age

☐ The future

☒ Sickness *Really for with*

☐ Old age

☐ Death

☐ Failure

I trust . . .

☐ Drinking/gambling (escape frustrations and boredom)

☐ Sex/pornography (pleasure, relief from cursed world)

☒ My own resources

☐ Security/peace

- ☐ Food
  (relief from boredom, health, pleasure, peace)

- ☐ Some idealized figure
  (athlete, pastor, musician)

- ☐ Inheritance, insurance, possessions
  (for security)

- ☐ Sickness
  (control, attention, no responsibility)

- ☒ My job
  (security, status, financial gain)

- ☒ My kids, job, marriage (for happiness)

- ☐ Pleasure (food, drink, drugs, sex, fun)

- ☐ Physical appearance (fitness, fashion, beauty)

- ☒ My gifts/abilities

- ☒ Control/order

- ☐ Luxuries

- ☐ Status

- ☒ Money

I desire . . .

- ☒ To feel good (eat, drink, drugs, sex, TV)
- ☒ Freedom from financial constraints
- ☒ Adoration/recognition/success
- ☒ That my children be responsible
- ☒ Any one of God's blessings!
- ☒ That my spouse and friends love me
- (☐) That circumstances be different
- ☒ Competence and affirmation

- ☒ Pleasure/comfort
- ☒ Peace in my home
- ☒ Love from others
- ☒ Material goods
- ☒ A nice house
- ☒ Knowledge
- ☒ Approval
- ☒ Health

Allow up to five minutes for group members to work through this list, and then regain everyone's attention.

Let's open this deeper part of our study by discussing an example that's common to many of us.

4. Thinking about the idol "love" of money," how would you know it's become an idol in your life? What would be the evidence that money has created an excessive desire, trust, or fear within you?

— hoarding
— sin to get it
— not sharing

necessary
not idols

5. As much as you're willing, share about one of the other items you checked off. What's the evidence that this has become, or could become, an idol in your life?

health — depleats $ for life

Very often, what seem like "harmless" sins on the surface hide a much larger idol. For example, behind a juicy item of gossip may be an idol of reputation, a love of status, or a desire for revenge. One reason we need to discover our "subterranean" sins is that if we only repent of the surface "weed" instead of the "root" sin, it will keep growing back again and again.

Before we look more closely at our own lives, let's go to some biblical examples of idolatry and realize that we're far from alone in these struggles.

Subdivide into four groups (a group of "one" is okay). Assign one of the following to each group: Genesis 20:1–13; 1 Samuel 15:10–24; Acts 5:1–11; Mark 14:66–72 with Galatians 2:11–14 (both passages).

6. Read the assigned verses, and then discuss the following questions:

a. What's the surface sin here? In other words, what's the sin everyone sees?

b. What external circumstance set it off? What "pushed" those in your passage to commit this sin?

c. What hidden idol in their hearts—what threat to their old identity—does this sin reveal?

After ten minutes, bring everyone back together. Ask for a volunteer from each group to share the group's insights.

> *"You have made us for yourself and our hearts*
> *are restless until we find our rest in you."*
> — Saint Augustine

Surface sins call our attention to what's really going on inside us. When we have a wandering eye, this should be a red flag indicating a lusting heart. Boasting is a red flag indicating an underlying idol of self-glorification. Anger, another red flag, alerts us to any number of failed idols. What's more, by trusting our idols we're not just trusting in other things—in essence we're trusting ourselves instead of God. We use our idols to place ourselves on the throne and set ourselves up as false gods.

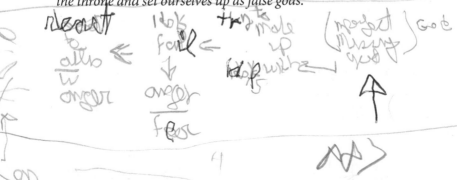

Extreme statements (handwritten)

OPENING YOUR LIFE

20 MINUTES

We've trained our eyes by looking at the examples of Abraham, Saul, Ananias and Sapphira, and Peter. Now it's time to look at our own examples. What are the false expectations we put on others, and what do they say about the hidden idols in our own hearts?

X must (handwritten)

Read through the list below. Some of these examples are humorous, some not, but all point toward potentially deeper issues in our lives. Check off any items where you think, that's me! Take ten minutes to work through this on your own, and then we'll discuss more together.

☐ When I talk to people, they must give me their undivided attention. (People must respect me.) *get off phone* (handwritten)

☐ People must not mess around with me or catch me off guard. (I control my world. Things must be ordered. Things must not break down or mess up.)

☐ I have the right to judge others. (Especially externals, because I cannot see into their hearts. I judge their shortcomings and sin. I compare myself favorably with them.)

☐ I speak and it is done (Genesis 1:1–31). (If things are not accomplished immediately, I am angry or defeated. My desire to change things rules me.)

☐ People need to stay out of my way on the road. (They must respect my wishes. I should have control of how I drive.)

☐ People must obey me. (That goes double for my children.)

☐ I have to be right. (Thus I defend, attack, condemn, adjust the record, destroy others' records, excuse, build good karma, blame.)

☐ I glorify myself. (I am all-knowing, all-wise. I look down on others' mistakes; my opinions are all-wise and correct.) *I oughta* (handwritten)

☐ I do whatever pleases me. (TV, food, sex, shopping, entertainment, videos, computer games, vacations.)

☐ I have to look holy. (I have to appear perfect. I am Dr. Jekyll at church, but Mr. Hyde appears at home. There's also a good chance I'm involved in church leadership—or at least have an unusually strong opinion about the job the church leaders are doing.)

☐ If you call me to account I get mad or raid the fridge. (I am accountable to no one.)

☐ I must be healthy. (I have a right to good health.)

☐ I must be independent. (I must not depend on anyone.)

☐ People must love me. (I want to be loved by…)

☐ People must serve me. (They must meet my "need.")

☐ People must not look at me. ("He dissed me so he had to die"—an actual statement from a criminal in New York City who had just shot someone.)

☐ Life revolves around me. (I must be the center of my family life, my job, my church.)

☐ I must make it to the top. (I must win—job, sports, computer games. I aim for the top and will tread over anyone to get there.)

☐ I get vengeance. (I don't get mad, I get even or I freeze people out.)

☐ I must save (myself, my spouse, children, friends) from their sinful behavior, and so on. I must bring peace. (I never argue. I bring good tidings.)

☐ I make my own laws or rules for living. (As the commands of God are an expression of God's character, so my laws are an expression of the character of my idolatry.)

Some of my laws include:

☐ The toothpaste tube must be squeezed from the bottom. The soap must not be broken in two. (I control my world.)

☐ I read the newspaper first. (People must honor me.)

☐ The house has to be tidy. The food must be good. (People must serve me. People must compliment me. People must not see me as a slob.

"Please excuse the mess" when there is no mess. If my house is together, then I am together.)

☐ The toilet paper must come over the top so it does not rub against the wall and get dirty. (I demand cleanliness.)

☐ The toilet paper must come from underneath so we use less of it. (I demand thriftiness.)

☐ The family must be ready on time. (I demand respect. I would hate for people to see me late.)

☐ Make your own rule: _____

After ten minutes, regain everyone's attention.

7. Again, as much as you're comfortable doing so, share about one or two of the items you checked. What made you say, that's me! How surprised were you by the underlying sin that went with the statement—and do you agree with it? Explain.

8. How does this behavior indicate that you're still leaning on your old identity, instead of your new identity in Christ?

The difference between trusting idols and trusting Jesus is like the difference between drinking seawater and drinking fresh water. Two things happen when you drink seawater: you get thirstier, and you start to go crazy. Idolatry is like that. Your view of reality becomes warped. Something that seemed so wrong in the past is now acceptable. Worse still, the more you drink, the thirstier you become. A false god is just that—false. It promises life, but instead brings death. Only Jesus is living water—fresh water that quenches our thirst.

Have group members get into pairs.

Chances are, today's study has brought up some ongoing idols in your lives, whether they're ones you haven't recognized before or ones you wanted to forget. But as we learned in our last session, we need to give God the chance to deal with the sins that keep cropping up in our lives, no matter how tired we are of dealing with them.

One of the best ways to stop serving idols is to serve others instead; it's a great way to get our minds off us. The options below include a couple ideas to get you thinking in that direction. But again, if God has prompted you to do something else as a result of our time today, do that!

No matter what you decide, in the space that follows write down the one thing you'll do this week to make today's session more real in your own life. Take ten minutes to share your commitment with your partner, and make plans to connect with each other before the next session. Then close your time together in prayer. Thank God for uncovering the idols in your lives, and ask for his strength and grace to remove them from your lives.

When you're done praying, stay quiet or move into another room to give other pairs a chance to share and pray together. May God remove every idol in your lives so that you can receive every new blessing he wants to give you!

- You might still be struggling with identifying your idols. So here's a tough but rewarding assignment: sit down with a trusted friend and ask him or her to be brutally honest with you about the things you place between yourself and God. Don't defend yourself; just listen. Accept that the truth will hurt, but that it's a step toward deliverance. Be sure to end your time together with as much prayer as you need.

- Develop the habit of giving others credit or praise for a job well done, no matter how big your role might have been or how seemingly small theirs was. And if praise comes your way, accept it humbly and thankfully—don't add to it. Practice becoming the *non*-center of attention.

- Is there something in your life you're giving way too much attention to? Give it away. If it's something you truly need and can't give away, find a way to share it with others—lend it out, use it together, but in any case use it to serve someone other than yourself.

This week I'm going to begin tearing down the idols in my life by:

budget

healthcare plan

Consider coming back together at the end of the session for another time of worship. This time, worship as long as you desire!

IT'S ALL (NO LONGER) ABOUT ME

OVERVIEW

In this session we'll better recognize how self-centered, rather than Christ-centered, we are, and the different ways our self-centeredness is displayed and can be addressed.

This session and the previous one are essentially two different perspectives on the same thing: our self-centeredness and unbelief. Nevertheless, it's helpful to make a distinction. We resort to idolatry *because* we are looking out for number one. We *do* because we *are*, and what we *are* is deeply selfish. Self is at the center of our idolatry. Some areas to examine concerning the "self" are:

self-justification	self-discipline	self-glorification
self-righteousness	self-destruction	self-motivation
self-gratification	self-deception	self-loathing
self-regard	self-love	self-pity

This session focuses on three "self" attitudes and behaviors in particular: (1) self-generated righteousness, (2) self-deception, and (3) self-pity. We'll also examine the seemingly contradictory but very real connection between legalism and license, and how both ultimately stem from self.

OPENING THE DISCUSSION

15 MINUTES

*We're going to jump right in today because, after all, this session **is** all about us. Our first question tackles a serious issue, but let's try not to take ourselves too seriously as we discuss it. After all, most of us have probably been guilty of some of these at one time or another. Take a minute or two to review the list below, and then we'll discuss each form of "righteousness."*

Health-righteousness: You're not eating well. I had better enforce my dietary habits on you.

Language-righteousness: You used the word *fortunate*, or *lucky*. (Don't you believe in the providence of God?) You keep on splitting the infinitive. You ended a sentence with a preposition!

Holiday-righteousness: How on earth can you do that on Christmas, Easter, Halloween, and so on?

Entertainment-righteousness: You put your TV in the center of your living room, play computer games, and watch videos. This indicates that you are worshiping entertainment.

Finance-righteousness: How could you spend your money on that? I would never do that. You do not manage your finances as well as I do. This could have been given to the poor (Judas).

Theological/Ideological-righteousness: How could you possibly hold that view?

Political-righteousness: I can't believe you voted for…

Kids-righteousness: You have such poorly behaved children. I am clearly a better parent than you.

My-righteousness: How dare you criticize me!

Anti-Pharisee–righteousness: Why are you so dull, condemning, and judgmental? I would *never* judge someone like that.

Idea-righteousness: Why can't you think of anything original? Here's how *I* get righteous (add your own idea here): _____

_____

1. Which of these best represents the way you "get righteous" on others? How do *you* say it when it happens?

[handwritten: tell your my idea]

[handwritten: my belief]

[handwritten: questions about your idea]

[handwritten: want the better]

We love being right and looking good—pretending that we're better than we really are. We also love pretending that the people around us are far more messed up than we are—this way we've given ourselves permission to yell at them, shame them, criticize or crush them. But if we stop and think about it, we know our righteousness isn't any kind of righteousness at all, let alone God's kind. So let's give each other some grace here as we explore what to do about all this righteousness that comes purely from self.

OPENING THE WORD

We're going to look at three ways we focus on self—self-righteousness, self-deception, and self-pity.

Ask for one or more volunteers to read Luke 11:37–54. Then discuss the following questions:

2. What specific acts of self-righteousness does Jesus accuse the religious leaders of, and why are they wrong?

[handwritten notes]
34 attorhon - cleen outsbll
42 gue things not kore
43 status
46 lawyers burden quiet

3. What acts does Jesus tell them to do instead? Why those in particular?

[handwritten notes]
cleen inside
give love
nork with the Lold fnd aeil

Read Romans 1:18–32, and discuss the following questions:

4. What does this section of Romans (especially verses 18–21) tell us about the origins of our self-deception?

18 hinder the truth clearly seen
21 become vain & senseless

5. How does self-deceit lead to the more outward sins described in verses 28–31?

28 refused to have God in their knowledge

Ask for volunteers to read John 12:3–8; Luke 22:3–6; and Matthew 27:1–5. Then discuss the following:

6. How does Judas slide into a state of self-pity and despair over the course of these three passages? What was at the core of this downward slide?

6 - Judas was a thief
sat an entered into Judas
conspired & committed to sell betray
repented hung

No matter what direction self-centeredness pulls us, it pulls us away from Christ. Another way to view the self is to recognize that it moves back and forth between legalism and license. Although outwardly they look like opposites, at heart they are the same thing. Both involve looking after self; both are idolatrous; both betray our true identity in Jesus.

The table, "Birds of a feather," explores some of the differences and similarities between legalism and license. Take a couple minutes to read through, and then let's discuss it.

Figure 8.1

Birds of a Feather

	legalism	license
feels good	It feels good to be right, to be better than others.	It feels great to raid the fridge, to indulge.
feels bad	I despair when my righteousness is undermined, when I am exposed as a fraud.	I despair when my family, or my body, is ruined by my indulgence.
looks good	Because I am right, and better than others, I look good.	My habits regarding vacations, recreation, sleeping, and eating show I look after my body well.
looks bad	Gossip, anger, criticism, frowning looks.	Drunkenness, gambling, drugs, laziness.
self-justification	To remove guilt and to look right, I do things that look good.	To remove guilt, I indulge myself. i do things so I can reward myself with indulgence.
self-glorification	I use my deeds to gratify my boastful heart. I criticize others to glorify myself.	My lustful imagination uses other people to worship me. I don't care what others think' I enjoy a scandalous reputation.
self-deception	I am right. Therefore, I cannot be wrong!	I am not addicted. I can beat this. This does not harm anyone.
self-gratification	I use other people for my pleasure. Their admiration gratifies my heart.	I use other people for my pleasure, e.g., sexual lust. I use pleasures to gratify my heart.

© 2006 World Harvest Mission

7. Regardless of which side—legalism or license—"felt better" to you, *why* do these behaviors appeal to us? Share a personal example, if possible.

8. What are we saying to Jesus when we engage in *any* of the self-centered behaviors we've discussed?

it all about me

"Everybody thinks of changing humanity and nobody thinks of changing himself."
— Leo Tolstoy

OPENING YOUR LIFE

Subdivide into pairs (a trio is okay if you have an odd number of group members).

*The root of pride is your old self—the self that wants to be in charge of your own life instead of submitting to Jesus. By its very nature, pride does not—will not—see itself, let alone its own sin. Instead, in the grip of pride we become insistent and demanding in our relationships with others. After all, **they're** the ones who are wrong and who should honor **our** wishes.*

"You were taught, with regard to your former way of life, to put off your old self, which is being corrupted by its deceitful desires; to be made new in the attitude of your minds; and to put on the new self, created to be like God in true righteousness and holiness" (Ephesians 4:22–24).

Once you've read Ephesians 4:22–24, talk over the questions that follow with your partner. You'll be coming up with your own challenges this week in response to what God's brought up during this session, so be sure to also set aside some time this week to touch base with your partner and encourage one another. Let's plan to come back together in ten minutes.

9. Where in your life are you still trying to hang on to your old self? Be honest with each other about what "deceitful desires" you are still struggling with.

reputation
prepore & rehecore

10. What's one practical way you can put off your old self so you can be made new in Christ? Write your answer below, and share it with your partner.

This week I'll hand over my self-centered old self to Jesus by:

After ten minutes, get back together.

Invite people to share their discoveries and needs with the larger group, but don't pressure anyone. Then—because it *is* no longer about you—open up your prayer time to the entire group. Open and/or close your time—or ask for volunteers to do both—but make this time about lifting up each others' needs, praising God for who he is, and thanking him for what he's already done in your lives. Ask God to reveal to each group member how to let go of self and embrace him instead. Take as long as you need, and lay down every crown before our almighty and loving God.

ADDITIONAL NOTES:

AM I *REALLY* A NEW CREATION?

OVERVIEW

In this session we'll recognize how the Spirit is already working in our lives and that we are no longer defined by our sins, even as we continue to address them.

What would I discover about you if I had the opportunity to know you as you really are? When people are asked this question, they usually give a pessimistic answer. Many people tend to view themselves negatively when asked to talk honestly about their "real" self. And as we've seen throughout this study, there's good cause for that. One problem, of our own creation, is defining ourselves by our sins, problems, bad habits, successes, and failures.

But as we've also hopefully discovered, that's not the whole story, let alone the most important part. This session unpacks a much bigger truth about us—that our real identity is not defined by our sin but by Christ, and that he is actively helping to make us into the people we were created to be all along. We are still sinners, but our true identity is in Christ. Let's learn together how to live in the reality of that new identity.

OPENING THE DISCUSSION

15 MINUTES

1. About whom in your life do you most use the phrase: "He/She's a saint"? Why do you say that about him or her?

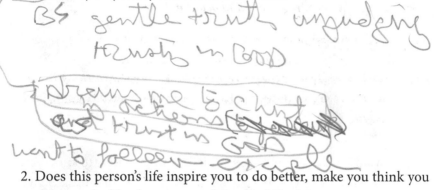

handwritten annotations: BS gentle truth unjudging trust in God; draws me to Christ ... trust in God; want to follow example

2. Does this person's life inspire you to do better, make you think you could never be like that, or something else? Explain your answer.

handwritten annotations: will do better / able to trust God in God

No one is born a saint. Even our best behavior is not what makes us saints. Rather, Jesus' sacrifice on our behalf, and our receiving the new life he offers us, is what accomplishes that. And as we walk closer and more consistently with Jesus, we begin to bear a closer outward resemblance to the new identity we already have on the inside.

*Although we are already new creations in Christ, we still have unbelief to overcome. We forget who we really are; we define ourselves by our successes and failures, rather than by what **God** says we are. It's true: the works of the flesh still need to be repented of. But it is no longer I who lives, but Christ who lives in me (Galatians 2:20)!*

Who am I? Saint or sinner? These two things are not on an equal footing or equal reality (1 John 3:9, 14; 5:18). Saint wins hands down! The sinner is there, but that is no longer my true identity (Romans 8:9). Because of this, we can gladly choose to view both ourselves and other Christians in this manner. We can enjoy constructive relationships with others that are characterized by encouragement and peacemaking.

Since your next session will be your last one, you probably want to start discussing what to do after you've completed this study. Will you move on to one of the other two Gospel Transformation studies, *Gospel Growth* and *Gospel Love*? Study another subject? Make plans now, if you haven't already.

OPENING THE WORD

35 MINUTES

*Before working on the sinner mindset, let's realize we all start from the same place—we **are** sinners. **All** of us. The apostle Paul considered himself the "worst" of sinners (1 Timothy 1:15). And yet he regularly refers to the church around him as "saints" (e.g., Romans 1:7; Ephesians 1:1). How is this possible? Let's look closer at his example and see what we can learn from it.*

Read aloud Philippians 3:3–17. Then discuss:

3. From a human standpoint, what "successes" does Paul have before encountering Christ? Where was he really, from God's perspective?

4. On the other hand, in what ways can you say, as Paul does here, Follow my example (v. 17)? No false modesty here. What has Christ taught you that you wished everyone knew as deeply? How does it prove that your new identity in Christ is real?

> "To 'grow in grace' means to utilize more and more grace to live by, until everything we do is assisted by grace. . . . The greatest saints are not those who need less grace, but those who consume the most grace, who indeed are most in need of grace—those who are saturated by grace in every dimension of their being. Grace to them is like breath."
> — Dallas Willard, *Renovation of the Heart*

Whether we think too highly or too little of ourselves, we are nonetheless thinking in the flesh instead of the spirit—out of our old identity instead of our new one. The two cycles laid out on the following pages describe two conflicting belief systems that can define "me," my self-perception, who I believe I am as a person.

Take a few minutes to review the two illustrations, "Vicious cycle of unbelief" and "Gracious cycle of faith," or take turns reading the sections. Then discuss the questions that follow.

P67

1 How I See Myself

- I am focused on sin and self.
- I am focused on my successes and failures.
- I see my idols, lust, anger, pride, gossip, laziness, bad relationships, etc.
- Satan's accusations sizzle and burn.

- I conclude: "This is who I really am."
- My sins, problems and bad habits define me.
- My successes and/or failures define me.
- I wonder why Paul doesn't start his letters, "To all the sinners in...; unholy and disobedient...; anger from God our Judge."

2 How My Heart Responds

THE VICIOUS CYCLE OF UNBELIEF

Who I am in my flesh is foremost in my heart and mind. Who I am in Christ seems faint and unreal.

4 How I See Others

- I project my view of myself onto other Christians.
- Like me, their sin also defines who they are.
- I gossip about them.
- Who they are in Christ is incidental.

3 My Spiritual Focus

- At the exposure of my sin I am despondent.
- I try to avoid the pain of exposure by covering up my sin.
- I forget who I am in Christ.
- I give intellectual assent to who I am in Christ but it is "only positional," it will really be true only when I get to heaven.

Figure 9.1

1 How I See Myself

- I am focused on Jesus.
- I see: Christ and his righteousness, perfection, obedience, and the Father's delight in him. I rejoice in these gifts! I am a new creation.
- Satan's accusations fizzle in the sea of the gospel.

- I conclude: 'This is who I really am!'
- Christ's righteousness, obedience, and perfection define me.
- I know why Paul starts his letters, "To all the saints in...; holy and faithful...; grace and peace from God our Father."

2 How My Heart Responds

THE GRACIOUS CYCLE OF FAITH

Who I am in Christ is foremost in my heart and mind. His righteousness and perfection define me.

4 How I See Others

- I view other Christians the same way.
- Like me, Christ's righteousness defines who they are.
- Their sins are incidental to my view of them.
- I am able to love and forgive others.
- Because I love others, I share the gospel with them.

Figure 9.2

3 My Spiritual Focus

- I am filled with joy.
- My heart-belief: "I am perfect and accepted."
- Based on this truth, I can now admit to the flesh instead of hiding, revising the record, blaming, judging, trying to build "good karma," or indulging in sin. I repent of the sinful nature.
- Believing who I am in Christ leads me to repentance.

5. What sections or comments in each of these charts resonate most with you? Why?

P 67

6. How does what's going on inside us—whichever identity we're embracing—affect people around us?

as BS done P84

OPENING YOUR LIFE

30 MINUTES

Let's dig even deeper into our two cycles. Turn back to pages 87–88. This time we are not going to just identify a general problem. For each chart ("The Vicious Cycle of Unbelief" and "The Gracious Cycle of Faith") choose a particular example from your own life and describe it using categories 1 through 4 from each chart. Take five minutes to work through each of the next two questions by yourself. We'll debrief this exercise afterward, so try to choose examples you are comfortable sharing.

7. In each section below using the categories from the chart on page 85, write a short paragraph describing how you have recently fallen into a vicious cycle of unbelief in one area of your life.

Section 1 – How I See Myself

now all good – won't last

Section 2 – How My Heart Responds

worry fear anger

Section 3 – My Spiritual Focus

off target

Section 4 – How I See Others

part of problem or solution

After five minutes, regain everyone's attention and move on to the next question.

8. In each section below using the categories from the chart on page 86, write a short paragraph describing how you have seen the Spirit work the gracious cycle of faith in one area of your life.

Section 1 – How I See Myself   *SM*

servant is backup

Section 2 – How My Heart Responds

afraid then amazed

Section 3 – My Spiritual Focus

on God

Section 4 – How I See Others

all can

After another five minutes, regain everyone's attention once more. Ask group members to get into subgroups of three or four.

In your groups, share what God's revealed to you through this exercise, and then discuss the questions that follow. Next, think about how you'll respond to this session. Choose one of the challenges below—or whatever God has put on your heart to do. In the area below, write the one thing you'll do this week to make today's session more real in your life. Share your commitment with your partners, and make plans to connect with each other before the next session to encourage one another. Let's plan to regroup in twenty minutes.

9. What thoughts and emotions did you experience as you worked through each cycle? What does that tell you about the importance of embracing your new identity in Christ?

[handwritten] agreed to cycles
[handwritten] beautifully valued itself my self
[handwritten] — right path, continue with trust

10. What are some practical ways we can help break the cycle of unbelief and embrace the cycle of faith instead—and help others do the same? Come up with as many ideas as you can.

[handwritten] — accept it into own understanding
[handwritten] — test answers
[handwritten] — share experience + support with judgement

This week's challenges:

- Tell someone about your new identity in Christ and what that means to you. Be brave: if possible, find a non-Christian friend and tell that person that you'd appreciate his or her help. Ask for feedback. What made sense? What didn't? Answer any questions, and if there are questions you can't answer, promise to find out and report back.

- Who in your life is tough to love—someone you regularly exclude from your life? Do something to include that person. Invite him or her to lunch with you or a group of friends. Ask about his or her week, and *really listen* to the answer. Learn what Christ is doing (or trying to do) in that person's life, and take time to sincerely affirm it. Also, consider what it is in *you* that makes *that* person in particular so hard to embrace.

- Here's something to try either as a smaller group or a larger one: show Jesus' love in a concrete way to someone who needs it. Visit someone who's sick or shut in. Or maybe there's a home or car repair you can perform or help pay for. Take some time afterward to debrief as a group: how did demonstrating this kind of love affect your perception of the people you helped and people in general? Did it inspire you to do something else? If so, start planning your next act of love and service together.

This week I'll remember and express my new identity in Christ by:

____

____

____

After twenty minutes, get back together and close in prayer.

Thank Christ for the new life and new identity he's given you, and the opportunities he has given you to express that new identity outwardly. Ask the Spirit's help in catching each of you when you threaten to cycle into unbelief. Ask him to help you remember who you are in Christ and to continue walking in faith.

GROW FORWARD— AND OUTWARD

OVERVIEW

In this session you'll discover how your new identity in Christ expands your view of the world God created—and your influence upon it—as you serve God's creation more openly and outwardly.

Our new identity in Christ is not just for us. As we allow the light of Jesus to hit every part of our lives, it enables us to see past ourselves. We see past what God has done for us and begin to see something even more amazing—that our Creator has designed us to be part of his plan for transforming the world!

We not only receive blessings from Christ, but we also receive burdens for the people around us. We begin to develop the heart of Christ and to see opportunities to serve others. And as we become more and more like Christ, we *want* to serve—not only to make ourselves feel good, but for Christ's sake. Serving becomes not just something we do because "we have to," but a tangible way to grow further in Christ and with Christ.

OPENING THE DISCUSSION

15 MINUTES

Make sure you have a plan for next week and beyond. Also, have a plan for celebrating your completion of this study, and the work God's done in your lives through it. Do something special before or after your gathering time, or plan a separate celebration for another time and place.

Let's take some time today to reflect upon and celebrate what God is already doing in our lives, including what he's done in our lives through this study, so that we can prepare ourselves for the even better things he has in store for us.

1. Over the last few months, in what ways have you seen your new life in Christ and your "everyday life" intersect more?

2. How has that changed you? How has it challenged you?

As we've seen again and again during this study, Jesus wants our faith to be more deeply woven into every part of our lives. But it doesn't stop there. As we learned in our previous session, we're called to be Christ's ambassadors to the world (2 Corinthians 5:20)—to be a functioning piece of Christ's reconciling work here on earth. So let's spend our final session of this study expanding our view of our new identity in Christ.

> "If there's anything in life that we
> should be passionate about, it's the gospel . . .
> passionate in thinking about it, dwelling about it,
> rejoicing in it, allowing it to color the way
> we look at the world."
> — C. J. Mahaney, *The Cross Centered Life*

OPENING THE WORD

On your own or taking turns as a group, look over and read through the two illustrations on the following pages. Here's what each represents:

- *"Tunnel vision"* illustrates what happens when we lose sight of the gospel story—what God has done, is doing, and will do in the future.

- *"20/20 vision"* illustrates what we aim for in the Christian life— a growing appropriation of the gospel to every part of our lives.

After you've worked through and feel you understand these two illustrations, move on to the questions that follow.

Figure 10.1 — TUNNEL VISION

1. Figure 10.1, **Tunnel Vision,** represents us, operating out of our pride and unbelief, which narrows and blurs our vision. Thus, our grasp of both the cross/gospel (Section 2) and our heart's condition (Section 3) is impaired.

2. The **cross** represents the gospel. Because of our poor vision, our perception of the gospel is fuzzy and limited—perhaps we see it for only a moment and then quickly forget about it. Here we see only a small part of the gospel, for example, the forgiveness of our sins. To whatever extent we walk in pride, unbelief, and self-reliance, we will suffer tunnel vision, and the benefits of the gospel will grow dim and distant to us.

3. The **heart** is the operating center of our being, and a mixture of both good and bad. Because of our poor vision, it is difficult to see our heart's attitude and direction. Here we see only a small part—for example, an unforgiving or forgiving spirit toward others.

4. The **Spirit** gives us light, power, and life. Because of our unbelief and pride we are less under the influence and power of the Spirit. We see less of the life Christ intended for us. Without the Spirit we cannot see God or ourselves correctly. Neither can we change, grow, or even love other people.

Figure 10.2 — 20/20 VISION

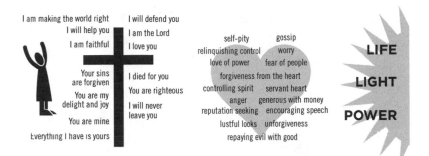

1. Figure 10.2, **20/20 Vision,** represents us as we open our eyes and hearts in faith to what God has done, is doing, and will do. It also opens our eyes to what we are really like. Faith includes accepting that what God says about us is true, and rejecting incorrect views of ourselves. This other dimension of faith could be called repentant faith.

2. The **cross** represents the gospel—all that God has done and is doing through Jesus. As we walk in faith and repentance we can see more of the riches of the gospel—for example, our new status and identity become clearer. As we grow in knowledge of the gospel and of Jesus, we grow in a true knowledge of ourselves.

3. The **heart** is the operating center of our being, again a mixture of both good and bad. However, as we grow, our heart's attitude and direction become clearer to us. In addition, we are to view the good things we do through the lens of the cross. The cross undermines any boasting on our part, for through it we recognize that everything we have has been given to us.

4. The **Spirit** gives us light, power, and life. He shows us Jesus, gives us every spiritual blessing, and reveals to us our heart's condition. The Spirit also empowers us to live the Christian life, for we have no power in and of ourselves to do so.

3. In your own words, explain the four pieces of the two "Vision" graphics. How do they work together?

— Remember being a new
christian, help relate now

4. When have you experienced a significant case of either tunnel vision (where self was keeping you from seeing all God had for you) *or* 20/20 vision (when God opened your eyes *wide*)? Either way, how did it affect the way you saw God, yourself, and the world around you?

*God wants to expand our vision to see, and experience, the Spirit intersecting with every part of our lives. God also wants to expand our borders—the places and people in our lives where the Spirit **can** intersect. Jesus wants us to carry his love to the rest of the world, but we first need to receive his love to do it. Let's explore a prayer that Jesus himself prayed specifically with us in mind.*

Ask for one or more volunteers to read John 17:9–26.

5. What did Jesus mean that we are to be "in the world" but not "of the world"? What does that look like? Be as specific as you can.

6. In what ways have you already seen Jesus' prayer answered in your own life?

7. Reread verses 20–23. Based on these verses and our diagrams above, how *can* we achieve the kind of unity Jesus prays for here, so that the world can truly see it?

we all be one in belief & love

OPENING YOUR LIFE

Ask for a volunteer to read Hebrews 12:1–3.

witnesses

8. How have you seen some of the things you've learned about in the study modeled by others—maybe even others in this group? How has it inspired *you* to keep running the race? (Or to really *start* running it?)

validation
amplification
unrelenting one every mercy ~ can't understand in my front

9. Who do you see as your "mission field" right now, whether it's one person or a given group of people? Put another way, who specifically is God expanding your heart toward?

who k brought into my path

10. How can this group support you as you take the next steps God is calling you to take?

Ask everyone to get into pairs. A trio is okay if you have an odd number of people in your group.

You've just thought of someone God has given you a heart for, so you already have your assignment for this week—and beyond. Now, with your partner, spend the next ten minutes in prayer. Pray for each other and for those God has put on your hearts. If you haven't thought of someone, or can't seem to narrow it down to one person or group, ask God for his wisdom and direction. James 1:5 tells us, "If any of you lacks wisdom, he should ask God, who gives generously to all without finding fault, and it will be given to him." Let's plan to come back together in ten minutes.

After ten minutes gather everyone back together.

*Let's close by making Jesus' prayer in John 17 our prayer. Close your eyes and think once more about the things Jesus asked God for. Realize he asked them for **you**, and that God has answered that prayer. As we pray, ask Jesus to help you believe that and to walk it out in the days—and years—to come.*

Close your time with a prayer something like this:

*Lord, we ask that you **don't** take us out of this world, but that you **do** protect us from the evil one as we go out into the world. You call us yours, and because of that, we don't belong to this world anymore. We have a new identity in you. Thank you again for that truth. Help it to become more real to us with each passing day.*

*Just as you sent Jesus into the world, you send us. Help us to appreciate the awesome privilege—and responsibility—that truly is. And just as Jesus gave himself as a sacrifice for us, help us to sacrifice ourselves for the sake of what others need—**you**. Help us, as your church, to be one so that the world sees and believes you came for them, too—that they will come to believe that you love them as much as you love us. Help us to remember how much you love each person you've created, and form us more and more into the people you want us to be. In Jesus' name, amen.*

LEADER'S GUIDE

These answers are suggestions, not definitive responses to the questions. That doesn't mean they're not helpful or accurate, but it does mean your group might come up with better—and very possibly, more personally relevant—answers. So don't rely on this guide to "feed the correct answers" to your group. That will only serve to short-circuit the impact of this course and undermine opportunities for growth in your group members' lives.

*On the other hand, the group might get stuck on one or more questions, especially depending on the maturity level of your members. In that case, we're here to help. But again, don't use these answers as a crutch or a shortcut; wrestle with the questions together as a group **first** before looking at these answers.*

If you choose to use these answers as part of your regular discussion, we suggest the following format:

1. Discover. First, come up with your own complete answers to the questions using the Scripture passages, session content, diagrams, and your own personal and collective encounters with Jesus as a springboard. You need to discover the answers for yourself to get the most out of this study. As group leader, be sure to facilitate this type of learning and discussion.

2. Direct. *Now*, review, study, and discuss the suggested answers and reflections at the back of the manual.

3. Rediscover. Once you've reflected on both your answers and ours, spend time as a group talking about further ideas or questions that arise. Return to your original answers and write down any new insights, thoughts, and applications.

Good luck! May God grow you together!

SESSION 1: FIRST, THE BAD NEWS . . .

1–2. Answers will vary.

3. In addition to (or among) the personal examples your group members come up with: war, the economy, crime, divorce, health issues, death, unemployment, financial pressures, church scandals, depression, addiction. Share details of a difficult situation or a minor frustration from your own life, and give a brief explanation of how you are applying or not applying the gospel to this situation.

4. Answers will vary. Encourage group members to expand their answers.

5. We usually think that only bad circumstances tempt us. Yet good things can tempt us to forget about God, to think that we deserve these blessings, and to compare ourselves favorably with others. Although Solomon had received so much, he still became what we would today call a sex addict.

6. Answers will vary.

7. To justify yourself is to use your thoughts, words, or actions to appear good. It is the unbelieving heart's tendency to perpetually build its record before self, others, and God. It is the heart's instinct to cover shame and guilt. Examples include defending yourself, boasting, minimizing the severity of your sin, making excuses, gossiping, or feeling superior to someone else. Again, when have you ever said, "It's not my fault!"?

The church of Sardis built a reputation on the things they thought they did well. You can do just about anything to build a reputation—have well-behaved children, keep a clean house, succeed at your job, homeschool the kids, get the latest tattoo, learn about some intricate subject (so that even intelligent people think you're smart), get a degree, go on a missions trip. We can do all of these things without faith, the Spirit, or any dying to ourselves. The emphasis is on you and not Jesus.

Leader, share a recent example from your own life when you sought to justify yourself. Also, point out the distinction between doing good things out of a sense of self-justification, and doing good deeds out of faith and love for God. For example, we can tithe to show we're "right" before God, our neighbor, and ourselves. We can also tithe because we believe all our wealth is a gift from God, that Christ has given us all things, and that God loves us and will never forsake us (Hebrews 13:5).

8. Self-justification is one of the great hindrances to the Christian life—in fact, to *receiving* that new life in the first place. As Jesus said repeatedly about the Pharisees and hypocrites who justified themselves by their religious actions, "I tell you the truth, they have received their reward in full" (Matthew 6:2).

9. Answers will vary. Encourage group members to come with some of their own answers, or to expand upon the answers here. Behind each excuse is an implication. These examples illustrate how good we are at justifying ourselves—that at the core of our hearts is the overwhelming desire to appear right, good, better, less angry, more patient, and so on, than we really are.

10. If we claim to be without sin, we make God out to be a liar and his word has no place in our lives. If we say that we have not sinned, then we are calling God untruthful and his word has no part of us. On the contrary, when we own up to our sins, we are saying, "Yes, Lord, I do want you in my life; I want your word to be part of my life."

It is a healthy thing to admit to being a sinner because that is who we are. This is one of the first steps in Christian growth—to die to excuse-making. It is to admit the truth about ourselves. It is to die to our desire for self-justification. After all, how can we change if we won't admit that anything is wrong?

11. Asaph struggles with the arrogance and prosperity of the wicked and with his envy of their way of life. They give no thought to God, and don't appear to *need* to. In short, Asaph wonders why he's trying to live a holy life when there appears to be no benefit. At the same time, in Psalm 73, verses 15–17, he acknowledges that this "eat, drink, and be merry" philosophy is not something you teach your children or others—that you would betray them by doing so.

Asaph recognizes that the whole matter of suffering and the prosperity of the wicked is something he will never figure out. He goes to God's temple, to the place where he can meet with God's people and listen to them. Here he receives and understands the final destiny of the wicked—an end not seen in this world but only in the next, and understood only by faith. He receives God's promises and accepts them as true, rather than relying on what his eyes tell him. Asaph concludes, The wicked are satisfied by their possessions; as for me, I am delighted with God.

12. Answers will vary. Encourage group members to open up further about the issues they share as they get into their smaller groups.

SESSION 2: . . . AND NOW, THE GOOD NEWS

1. Answers will vary.

2. Genesis 1 introduces God's story. It lays the foundation for what is to come and provides a framework for understanding the rest of the story. Despite our views to the contrary, we are not God! The original verdict regarding creation is that it was "good."

We have a special place in creation and God made us in his image. We are not God, but we are like him. The world was not always like it is today. Humanity was intended to take care of creation—to rule it on behalf of/ under God.

3. Adam and Eve fell away from God when they stopped trusting and relying on him. They stopped trusting in God's love for them and his provision of every good thing. They thought they were missing something—something outside their relationship with God that could bring them life in all its fullness. Instead of trusting God, they believed the words of the serpent. Consider that God forbade eating from only one tree; he gave them everything else. The purpose of this tree, among other things, was to teach them to trust God for everything, to listen to him, and to decide what is right and wrong based on God's word.

4. After Adam and Eve turn away from God, the first thing they do is seek to build and protect their own reputation by complaining, defending, and attacking. Adam wastes no time telling God that the whole problem developed because of "the woman you put here with me" (Genesis 3:12). In addition, they feel shame and fear (verse 10). They certainly feel guilty over what they have done (hence the excuses), but they also feel shame. Shame is a more profound feeling than guilt. Guilt is feeling bad about

something I've done. Shame is feeling bad about who I *am*. Adam and Eve realize that there is now something profoundly wrong with their souls. This leads to their hiding.

5. Answers will vary.

6. After the failure of Adam and Eve to rule, and after Israel's failure to rule, the hope was for God to establish once again his rule and kingdom. The good news is that God has done precisely that—he has sent his Son, Jesus, as King, Lord, and Savior. The final liberation of God's people has arrived. Jesus' coming inaugurates a reign of salvation, righteousness, restoration, and justice. He casts out demons, heals the sick, and forgives sinners. Hence, the New Testament often speaks of the "good news of the kingdom."

On the cross, Jesus accepts the pain of our rebellion. This one act of forgiveness brings us into a right relationship with God. God raises Jesus from the dead and seats him at his right hand—appointed as King. Jesus now rules until all things will be under his dominion. This good news of kingdom salvation is much greater than Israel ever expected—Jesus was given his name because he was to save his people from their sins (Matthew 1:21). It was a greater salvation than freedom from their Roman overlords—it was salvation from sin, death, fear, and Satan—a salvation from bondage, alienation, blindness.

7. Answers will vary.

8. Our response should be one of repentance and faith. These are the two essential ingredients of the Christian life. As the Puritan Thomas Watson put it, repentance and faith "are the two wings by which a Christian flies to heaven." God now calls us to live individually and corporately with the reality of Jesus as King, Lord, and Savior, and not trust other things to bring us life, meaning, or glory.

9. Answers will vary.

SESSION 3: GOD MAKES IT RIGHT

1. Answers will vary.

2. Answers will vary. But here's one to touch upon: we don't believe that we are justified and made whole in God's sight. By gaining others' approval and recognition we fill that hole—that gap in belief—that was meant to be filled by God only.

3. The answer does not lie in the different types of offerings. Cain, as one who farms, offers from his harvest. Abel, as one who tends sheep, offers from his flock. This is what we would expect. It is perhaps significant that in Genesis 4:3–4 we read that Abel brings the *very best* portions (the fat from the firstborn) to God. With Cain, we read that he brought from of his crops. Does this indicate where Cain's heart lies—that he did not offer God his best? Clearly in Hebrews 11:4 we see that *faith* is the key ingredient to Abel's acceptable sacrifice. Abel brings his offering with a heart relationship, a vibrant and active trust in God. Without such faith, it is impossible to please God (Hebrews 11:6).

4. Cain's reaction to God's displeasure at his offering speaks for itself, as does Cain's complaint that God's punishment for Abel's murder is more than he can bear. God questions Cain about Abel, and his surly response, "Am I my brother's keeper?" (Genesis 4:9)—just after having murdered Abel—is perhaps the most self-justifying response in the Bible. And yet, in its own way, not so far removed from, "And who is my neighbor?" (Luke 10:29).

5. Answers will vary. Sometimes we simply try to "one-up" the other person—in other words, make ourselves look superior by acting smarter, funnier, or holier. Other times we go for the jugular; we belittle others—maybe even slander or gossip about them—so that we look like "bigger people" in comparison.

6. Eternal life, righteousness, grace, justification, forgiveness. All blessings come to us because we are in Christ. He is our representative. He won, so we win.

7. There are three main elements to the doctrine of justification by faith: (a) I am completely forgiven; (b) I am declared completely righteous; and

(c) I can receive this verdict of "righteous" only by faith. God's forgiveness of our sin and his lavish acceptance of us are not based on either our good works or our gross failures. They are based on Christ's dying on the cross for our sins and on his being raised for our justification (Romans 4:25).

8. In light of the gospel, we need not preserve, maintain, or fight for our reputation, identity, status, life, or control. God is in control. We need to rest in and submit to this. He has given us a new identity and reputation. God declares us right. Usually, when I try to demonstrate that I'm right, I have moved away from this gospel foundation. We also have the status of children of God and he has given us his Spirit. There is glory restored to us as children of God. Why search for glory elsewhere?

9–10. Answers will vary. Consider also sharing your own answers before the rest of the group attempts it. Make sure your example is specific, detailed, and preferably recent. Here's one possible scenario—use it as an additional example, or as a discussion starter:

I was upset with my wife because she did something that I asked her not to do. I felt disrespected. I told her I was upset, but the truth was that I was full of anger. In fact, I despised her. Moreover, because I believed she did something wrong, it felt right to harbor these evil thoughts. I concealed the truth in my heart by not naming my anger and contempt. Of course, as I preserved my own reputation and appearance, I could not admit my own sin or ignorance. Thus, I was far better at seeing my wife's "speck of sawdust" than my own "plank" (Luke 6:41–42).

As we believe the gospel, we stop defending ourselves. Along with the apostle Paul, we can own Galatians 6:14. Paul's boast is in the cross. It is his food and drink. Yet many times it is not our food and drink. This is especially clear when our spouse comes to us about something. We want to make sure the record gets set straight. How many times, when we are confronted with our sin, do we lash out and punish others, defend ourselves and accuse others, or internalize the pain and go into a kind of depression?

It is difficult to believe that God loves me despite my poor performance and gross failures, especially since I do not have this kind of love toward others. Believing that God has forgiven all my sins and has declared me righteous encourages the belief that God really does love me. Believing that God gave his one and only Son to bear my sins is the bedrock for believing that he does love me.

11. There are times when it may be proper to defend ourselves, but these times are less frequent than we think. We should ask ourselves why we respond so quickly. Why so intensely? Why do our minds simply go blank except for the desire to protect our own righteousness and make sure that our spouse, friend, coworker, or neighbor really understands "the whole picture"? Why do we mull, for hours or even days, over our response to someone and how to explain exactly what happened?

12. In the gospel, I am declared righteous. I am a child of God. Thus, I already have a perfect reputation, status, attainment, and appearance. In light of the gospel, I can admit my anger and repent of it. Thus, I no longer need to respond to others' self-justification with my self-justification. The gospel tells me that I too am forgiven an unimaginable debt, which when believed, frees me to love others (Luke 7:47). If I cannot believe that God loves me despite my own poor performance and gross failures, how will I ever be able to extend that love to others?

SESSION 4: JOIN THE FAMILY

1–3. Answers will vary. Have your own answers ready to share with the group, especially for question 3. By sharing the connection between your own perceptions of your earthly and heavenly fathers you'll help others make the connection as well.

4. The following are possible answers :

- When we call on the name of the Lord, he saves us (Acts 2:21).
- The Spirit testifies with our spirit that we are God's children (Romans 8:16). He made us sons and daughters; therefore, I'm part of a family that will last forever. Nothing will separate me from God's love (Romans 8:39).
- We are given an everlasting example in Jesus. And more and more, we bear the family resemblance (Hebrews 2:11).
- The redemption Christ earned for us, the Spirit applies to our hearts and lives. The Spirit enables us to accept our adoption by faith, and enables us to give expression to it by addressing God

as our Father (Galatians 4:6).

- We are no longer slaves to sin (Galatians 4:7). The Spirit gives us power to overcome evil. Jesus redeemed us from sin, death, the power of Satan, fear, the Mosaic law, and the basic principles of this world (Hebrews 2:14–15).
- God has made us coheirs with Jesus. As children of God, we share in what Jesus has (Romans 8:17).

5. Answers will vary.

6. Answers will vary. If some in your group say they are not anxious about anything, ask them what they think about when they have time to let their thoughts wander, and what happens after they do. What do they fear in their relationships, health, or finances? Some people recognize anxiety by feeling a knot in their stomach or a general irritability. Perhaps a friend or spouse could help them answer this question.

In addition, it may be helpful to note that not all fears or concerns are a bad thing. For example, fear of an abusive spouse is a good thing. We are addressing fears and worries that come from a lack of faith and a reliance on ourselves.

7. Our anxiety exposes our fear—a trust in ourselves to control our world, to orchestrate peace, security, love, etc. It exposes areas where we are trying to manage our lives apart from dependence on the love and sovereignty of God. It exposes our lack of trust in our Father to take care of us and give us grace to live well. When we are anxious, we are putting confidence in ourselves rather than in his love. Anxiety hinders our fellowship with God. It reveals our self-centeredness by exposing our ambitions, demands, expectations, and commitment to having our own way. Anxiety is a great indicator of where we are not believing the gospel and where we are not trusting Jesus.

8. We can yield or submit to the Father. As we go to him with our fears and anxieties, he corrects our view of reality. We are to believe that he controls our world and is for us. Sometimes we might need to face the worst-case scenario and realize that because God's grace is sufficient, we can trust him even if our situation does not change. God can be trusted because he is trustworthy. The story of our lives is only a small part of his great story. We do not know all the purposes that God has for us in

his story. However, he cares for us and loves us, so our best response is to go to him with our fears and anxieties.

9. Understanding our position in God's family removes anxiety. Knowing that a loving, all-powerful God is our Father, we are freed from our own false perceptions of ourselves, and we are able to bear good fruit. We want to serve others and bring them into the family.

10. Because we *are* adopted, being leads to doing. The "doing" is a natural and expected reflection and outworking of our love for God, not an anxious seeking of approval. An inability to show love for one another is an indicator that we are not in full relationship with our Father.

11. Answers will vary. Use the closing time to bring accountability to those commitments; make them more than nice things we think about doing. Do them—together, whenever possible.

SESSION 5: A NEW LIFE IN CHRIST

1–2. Answers will vary.

3. By faith the Spirit unites you to Christ. The work of the Spirit is to unite you into the body of Christ (Romans 12:4–5), and to bring to you everything that Christ has. Of course, the Christian life is focused not on the blessings as such, but on Christ himself. Every blessing you have received is received by being united to Christ (Romans 8:39). Because you are in Christ, you receive everything Christ has—his perfection, his perseverance, his adoption, his resurrection (Romans 6:10-11), and his obedience. In Christ, all these blessings are yours.

4. Answers will vary. But here are a few to consider and share with your group.

- I am united to Christ by faith. The work of the Spirit unites me to Christ and brings to me everything that Christ has. It is a life of fixing our eyes on Jesus (Hebrews 12:2). It is lived by faith (Galatians 2:20–21), and it is life in the Spirit (Galatians 5:16, 25).
- I am justified by faith in Christ through the Spirit of sonship (Romans 8:15).

- I am adopted by faith in Christ through the Spirit who justifies (1 Corinthians 6:11).
- I am sanctified by faith in Christ through the sanctifying Spirit (1 Corinthians 6:11; 2 Thessalonians 2:13; Titus 3:5; 1 Peter 1:2).
- I am able to persevere by faith in Christ through the work and power of the Spirit. Every blessing I receive comes by my being united to Christ. Because I am in Christ, I receive everything Christ has—his perfection, his perseverance, his adoption, his resurrection, and his obedience. In Christ, all these blessings are mine.

5–6. Answers will vary.

7. No; God's truth is unchanging while our own thoughts and feelings might float this way and that. We can advise others—and ourselves—to stay true to the promises God has given us, both through his Word and his Spirit. We can act upon those truths even when we feel dry or pulled in other directions.

8–10. Answers will vary.

11. The following are examples for each:

- The gospel frees you from striving to build your own record, reputation, or righteousness. Christ has freed you from the bondage, power, and guilt of sin (Galatians 4:8–9). Your freedom in Christ liberates you from a life of labor under unlimited obligation, a life of self-justification, guilt, bondage to sin, despair, and death.
- You are a son or daughter with a new identity (Galatians 3:26; 4:6–7; 1 John 3:1). You no longer need to find acceptance through the opinions and standards of others. You no longer have to fear rejection or live for approval. Because you are adopted, you can now be honest with your Father about your sins, weaknesses, and failures.
- You are forgiven, accepted, and in a right relationship with your heavenly Father. Yet this righteousness is not yours, but God's (Philippians 3:9). This applies to other Christians as well—they too are forgiven, accepted, and right with God; therefore, we should no longer condemn them (Matthew 18:21–35;

Ephesians 4:32). Once we understand that we are justified in Christ, we can use our tongues for encouraging one another, instead of criticizing, boasting, judging, or condemning.

- Sanctification is not only a process, but also a definitive, once-for-all act. Sin is no longer your master; you no longer have to obey its desires (Romans 6:12–18). A prisoner of war mentality means you have forgotten your release from the fetters of sin. In Christ, there is nothing that can rob you of faith and obedience. Though temptations may remain with you throughout your life, they no longer enslave you.

- Now that you are united with Christ, you are part of a new family. We belong to each other (Romans 12:5). Christ has formed a new humanity. There is nothing holy about withdrawing from Christian fellowship (Ephesians 4:3–6). In fact, such withdrawal will cause a decaying spirituality, since Christian growth always involves community. A hermit has forgotten that he or she is part of a new community.

- You have been raised spiritually and will be raised physically. As Christ was raised, you too will be raised (Romans 6:5). Christ frees you from the fear and despair of death (Hebrews 2:15); your union with Christ ensures your resurrection. You will conquer death because Jesus has conquered death (Romans 6:9). So your labor is not in vain, and neither is your faith.

- The gospel delivers us from the mentality of freely indulging the flesh (Ephesians 4:22–24). Now, in Christ, there is nothing that you have to have. All things are yours (1 Corinthians 3:21), because everything belongs to Jesus, and you belong to him. Your heavenly Father has been pleased to give you the kingdom (Luke 12:32).

- In Christ, you have a new King and Lord—Jesus (Colossians 1:15–20). He is Lord, but you have to receive him by faith as Lord. In other words, you have to live by faith in Christ's Lordship and humble yourself under God's mighty hand (1 Peter 5:6). This puts an end to your false claims to lordship—your attempts to manipulate or control others and your world.

SESSION 6: SINNERS IN THE HANDS OF A LOVING GOD

1. Answers will vary.

2. The younger son was selfish and self-serving—to the point where he essentially wished his father dead so he could spend his father's inheritance on himself. It is sometimes argued how self-serving the son may or may not have been even upon his return, but he has nonetheless been humbled, become aware that his father's riches are still abundant, and realized that being his father's servant is still preferable to entirely serving himself.

3. What would happen if he fell a third time or even a fourth? Can you think of some besetting sin in your own life? What about that? God's forgiveness is not rooted in the quality of our repentance or in our ability to sustain outwardly right behavior over a long period. God's forgiveness is forever rooted in the death of Christ. By dying on the cross Jesus received in his body the pain and consequences of our sin. He took all our debts upon himself. The good news is that God doesn't leave us, but he always pursues us with this extraordinary love. This love is of such a magnitude that we cannot fully grasp it.

4. The father showed long-suffering patience, acceptance, reassurance, compassion, forgiveness, comfort, joy, passion, intimacy. He sought out both sons; he sought restoration of a loving relationship with both. He lavished his love on the younger son and was more than willing to do it for the elder son as well—if that son would only ask.

5. Answers will vary. Try to have your own story ready. Chances are, someone in your group needs to hear it.

6. Jesus, God's Son, is the sacrifice for atonement. This not only conveys the idea of forgiveness, but also the idea of the wrath or anger of God actually being removed. His death—the shedding of his blood—is the means of forgiveness, the way that the anger or wrath of God is removed from guilty sinners. All who rest by faith in Jesus are now at peace with God. Jesus has completely met the just demands of God on our behalf. We are no longer under God's wrath. There is now no condemnation for those in Christ (Romans 8:1).

7. Personal examples will vary. We seldom just come out and say that we believe God is angry with us. Instead, this belief usually expresses itself in terms of floating guilt and a vague sense that we should be doing more. Also, like Adam and Eve, we tend to hide ourselves from God after we've sinned. See answers to question 8 for a fuller exploration of this.

8. The following are two big reasons:

- Radical forgiveness is hard to believe. For many Christians a continuing struggle with some bad habit or besetting sin hinders an uninterrupted belief in justification and adoption. The habit may even be relatively insignificant, but we keep doing it. We occasionally repent for it but usually just mull over it, deny its seriousness, or try to forget it. We stop repenting because we think it's dishonest to keep going back to God over and over with the same sin. Since we do not forgive that way we cannot imagine that someone else would or could.
- Repeated repentance is humbling. To trust Jesus requires giving up other things we trust in. Repentance entails giving up our false trusts, evil desires, and fears. Perhaps we have heard that repentance means turning from sin and not doing it again. We feel that if we *genuinely* repented, we would not do that sin again. This view merely encourages hypocrisy and a life without repentance. We might even think that we're making a mockery of the cross by repeated repentance. In reality, we are making a mockery of the cross by failing to come to Jesus in faith and repentance. Surely, the blood of Jesus is powerful enough to handle repeated offenses. Repeated repentance is progress!

Leaders, this question encourages us to examine the resistance of our own hearts when it comes to returning to the Father as sinners. There are other answers than these two. These, however, seem to be central because they expose a weak or inadequate view of repentance, the Father's love for us, and our justification.

9–10. Answers will vary.

SESSION 7: YOU ARE WHAT YOU WORSHIP

1. God, the Lord and Creator of all, deserves our praise. Without God we are literally nothing, and we are next to nothing in comparison to him. God gives us good things and deserves our gratitude. When we lift up God, our own spirits our lifted. By truly and deeply worshiping God, we take the focus off ourselves and put it squarely back where it belongs. And, all "spiritual" answers aside, it feels good to lose one's self in worshiping God.

2. First of all, idolatry is a sin by the simple fact that God commanded the Israelites—and by extension, us—not to have other gods or idols. By worshiping idols of our own making, we turn away from the living God, and in so doing cut ourselves off from the only true source of life, intimacy, relationship, and spiritual power. An idol is anything that draws us away from relying on Christ. It is anything that we love more than we love Jesus.

3. The Israelites were all too ready to reject "this fellow Moses" (Exodus 32:1), God's appointed leader and prophet. They were tired of waiting for God to act, and so they created a "god" who would "act" on their behalf. And after creating this idol "they sat down to eat and drink and got up to indulge in revelry" (verse 6)—an intent that was no doubt already on their hearts even before creating the golden calf.

4. How we respond to different situations can often reveal our idolatry. For example, how do we respond to not getting a pay raise or bonus, losing a job, a stock market crash, a major unplanned expense (like the car breaking down or a hefty dental bill), losing some material possessions, or a family member overspending or hoarding. In other words, it is often when our idols are *blocked* that we become aware of their presence. When idols are blocked or frustrated our reactions are varied, but are usually accompanied by anger.

5. Answers will vary. As you work through this exercise, it will be helpful to expand on a number of points by using examples from your own life. By sharing from your own life you give others permission to be trans-

parent and vulnerable as well. Try to draw out from your group some examples from their lives.

6. Abraham (Genesis 20:1–13)
   a. Surface sin: lying
   b. External circumstance: people's expectations
   c. Hidden idol: fear of people; fear of pain and death

   Saul (1 Samuel 15:10–24)
   a. Surface sin: disobedience—not destroying the Amalekites
   b. External circumstance: people's expectations
   c. Hidden idol: fear of people; desire to look good

   Ananias and Sapphira (Acts 5:1–11)
   a. Surface sin: lying
   b. External circumstance: everyone else was giving
   c. Hidden idol: desire for self-glorification, wanting to look good

   Peter (Mark 14:66–72; Galatians 2:11–14)
   a. Surface sin: denying Christ; outward conformity
   b. External circumstance: fear of persecution
   c. Hidden idol: fear of people; desire to look good

7. Answers will vary. Also, it's okay for group members to disagree with the assessment of the underlying sin—especially if there *are* other reasons (and there might be). On the other hand, don't allow group members to remain in denial about their idols. Lovingly help them to confront those issues. Help them to articulate the problem in their own words, so *they* can see it's a problem.

8. We are guilty of trying to find ways to satisfy the thirst in our own souls apart from God, out of our own resources. Our idols temporarily ease our pain, but in the end leave us even thirstier. Idolatry is extremely difficult to part with because it appears to satisfy us as only the gospel can do. Our idols tell us that we are okay. Because they seem to "work" to some extent, we are deeply committed to them.

SESSION 8: IT'S ALL (NO LONGER) ABOUT ME

1. Answers will vary. A few more examples follow:

- "I'm busy" conveys my own importance, as well as possibly, "therefore, I don't have time for *you*."
- "This show/movie's stupid/boring" implies "and so are you—but at least *I'm* not."
- "Worry about your own job" could be a defensive response to someone else's legitimate concern, and well as a hint that "I'm a better worker than you."

2. The religious leaders clean the outside of the cup and ignore the filth inside. There is a foundational principle here: what motivates your heart is what is going to come out in your behavior in the way you act and the way you speak. However, no matter how much you deal with the outside, it is not going to clean your heart.

These leaders also love others to greet them in the marketplace and crave the most important seats in the synagogue. This all has to do with a love for reputation, honor, and respect.

In Luke 11:44, Jesus says, "Woe to you, because you are like unmarked graves, which men walk over without knowing it." In Numbers 19:16 the law said that anyone who touched a grave was ceremonially unclean for seven days. For this reason, the Jews tried as hard as possible to mark graves by whitewashing them. Jesus compares the Pharisees to these graves. They are the ones who were defiling people, and people didn't know it. These Pharisees, by their law-oriented way of life, pretense, hard hearts, and unbelief were defiling everyone they encountered.

In verse 46, Jesus says, "And you experts in the law, woe to you, because you load people down with burdens they can hardly carry, and you yourselves will not lift one finger to help them." Of course, the teachers of the law thought they were doing a great service to the people—ensuring everyone kept the Mosaic law, and adding a bunch more laws just to make sure people stayed on the straight and narrow. A person will impose incredible burdens on people if they believe that ultimately it is for their good—and thus "lovingly" crush them.

Building tombs for the great prophets was another way to impress people and build a reputation. People would surely think, "These Pharisees, they honor prophets, so they must be like the prophets of old." But Jesus, in verses 47 through 51, says that these teachers of the law and Pharisees will be held accountable for the blood of those prophets.

In verse 52 Jesus says, "Woe to you experts in the law, because you have taken away the key to knowledge. You yourselves have not entered, and you have hindered those who were entering." The religious leaders were to lead others to a genuine and true knowledge of God. They were in a privileged position. They knew a lot about God and his law. However, their pretense and hypocrisy had blocked people from genuinely knowing God in an intimate relationship.

3. In verse 41 Jesus tells the Pharisees "give what is inside the dish to the poor, and everything will be clean for you." Giving freely to others releases us from bondage to our possessions and our appearances. In verse 42 he tells them to continue tithing, but to stop "neglect[ing] justice and the love of God." By seeking God's righteousness and making that our priority, we let go of our own righteousness and the need to look good.

4. We do not worship God (Romans 1:21). We choose instead to worship something of our own making. Every day, in many different ways, we are still saying, "I don't need God. I can do it myself." Thus, we exchange the truth of God for a lie, and worship and serve created things instead of the Creator (Romans 1:25).

5. We suppress the truth even though it is clearly visible. We have become futile in our thinking; our hearts are darkened; we have become fools. This is what we are like by nature. Because of this we become increasingly blind to our own sin. There is a powerful deceptiveness to sin. We need to be constantly reminded that sin has the power to deceive us. Thus, we are called to encourage one another daily, lest we be hardened by sin's deceitfulness (Hebrews 3:13).

6. In these passages, we see Judas go from a position of self-righteousness that covers up his own greedy, adulterous heart, to an opportunity to fulfill that greed by betraying Jesus for money, to the realization and remorse over who he was actually betraying. Judas thus loses hope in his ability to help himself and has cut himself off from God's ability to help.

Therefore, Judas despairs and takes his life. Pride and unbelief were at the core of Judas' despair, leading him first to betray Jesus, and then later to go out into a field and hang himself. In his case, suicide is the pride of self-pity taken to its ultimate extreme.

7. Both legalism and licentiousness have enjoyable aspects, hence we indulge in them. However, they also bring curses into our lives and we despair when they don't bring the life and satisfaction they've promised. There are elements of self-justification, self-glorification, self-deception, and self-gratification in both areas.

8. My failures and my sins are so great that there is no hope for me. I am totally despairing of my ability to save myself. I am trusting in myself and my ability. Jesus is not enough for me, so I fill the holes with my own self-righteousness or self-indulgence (or again, both). Once again, pride (or "self" wearing the crown) is the foundation for all our self-centered behavior.

9–10. Answers will vary.

SESSION 9: AM I *REALLY* A NEW CREATION?

1–2. Answers will vary. They will also reveal a lot about each group member's current mind-set, which will help you know how to emphasize the portions of the session that are upcoming. Spend more time listening than trying to address people's thoughts and feelings at this point. Let the rest of the session, and *God's* perspective, speak before adding your own perspective.

3. Paul was a Pharisee's Pharisee; "circumcised on the eighth day, of the people of Israel, of the tribe of Benjamin, a Hebrew of Hebrews; in regard to the law, a Pharisee; as for zeal, persecuting the church; as for legalistic righteousness, faultless" (Philippians 3:5–6). And yet, when Paul encounters Jesus on the road to Damascus, all Paul's "good works" are refuted: "Saul, Saul, why do you persecute me?... I am Jesus, whom you are persecuting" (Acts 9:4–5). Paul himself comes to the same realization, and later expands on it: "I consider everything a loss compared to the

surpassing greatness of knowing Christ Jesus my Lord, for whose sake I have lost all things. I consider them rubbish, that I may gain Christ" (Philippians 3:8).

4. Personal examples will vary. The outward fruit of the Spirit in our lives is evidence of the new life of Christ growing within us. As our old identity is transformed, our new identity becomes more evident. Paul spoke freely about what God was doing in and through his life, without bragging. The Spirit reveals us as we are, leaving us with an honest, joyful awareness that God is at work in our lives.

5. Answers will vary.

6. We tend to define others by what's going on inside us. If we're in a cycle of despair, guilt, or shame, it's likely we'll view others through that lens. When we try to cover up our sins, it's more likely we'll just be hiding from others, living in fear of exposure. In the meantime, those around us will already sense something's wrong and view us as hypocrites, especially if they *know* what's wrong. Living in the cycle of unbelief makes us self-centered and performance-oriented with others; living in the cycle of faith makes us others-focused and relationship-oriented.

7. Personal examples will vary. Leaders, please try to come up with your own example that you would feel comfortable sharing with the group.

8. Personal examples will vary. Leaders, please try to come up with your own example that you would feel comfortable sharing with the group.

9. Answers will vary.

10. Most saints we know—including the ones we talked about in questions 1 and 2—are marked by a sense of modesty. They are aware that they are not good in themselves, but only in Christ are they "saints." We too have the capability to fully discover this in our lives. The awareness of sin in our lives, while painful, is an opportunity for God to work. As we are faithful to repent and entrust God with each matter the Spirit brings to our hearts, so God is faithful to restore and transform us into truly new creations in Christ.

SESSION 10: GROW FORWARD— AND OUTWARD

Leader, throughout this session group members will have the opportunity to share both the burdens God has been laying on their hearts and how much their fellow group members have meant (and will mean in the future) to them. Again, this is a time to celebrate what God is doing and that you've made it through this study together! Be sure to come with your own stories of how this group has been a blessing to you. Don't be afraid to single out people. In fact, try to share something about *everyone* in your group, if time allows.

1–2. Answers will vary.

3. Answers will vary, and that's okay. There's no magic formula that says "Yes, this is exactly how it happens." There is plenty of mystery in the process, since the Spirit, like the wind, blows where he pleases (John 3:8). However, we can describe various elements that are part of the process. Our answers should include at least the following two elements:

- The Spirit of God is the one who produces fruit in our lives. It is the Spirit who sanctifies us and produces fruit in our lives (Galatians 5:22–23).
- Repentant faith looks to (a) what God has done, particularly in the death and resurrection of Jesus; and (b) our heart to access its condition. There is a clear connection between the Spirit's work and our ongoing trust in Jesus. The great power of the Spirit, who raised Jesus from the dead, is also at work in those who believe (Ephesians 1:18–20).

4. Answers to the first part, especially, will vary. Through the cross, and through the work of the Spirit, God demonstrates his great love for us. This love gives us a firm foundation to look honestly at our lives and heart condition, and in doing so gives us a heart for the world around us. We are no longer superiors but in the words of Paul David Tripp, "people needing change helping people in need of change." The Spirit always desires to draw us into a more intimate relationship with God, and yet that intimacy propels us outward as we seek ways to express our love for God.

5. We are called to be separated unto Christ, but not to separate ourselves from a world that needs to hear of, and experience, his love. Conversely, we are called to be servants of the world *because* of our allegiance to Jesus. Thus, our acts are to be Spirit led, not showy or compromising to our faith. Our examples will vary, but all should reflect God's calling upon our lives and the servant heart of Jesus.

6. Answers will vary.

7. Only by looking at Jesus can we hope to achieve the unity (not conformity) we seek to experience within the church, and even within our group. Christ will never lead us into a spirit of disunity, gossip, distrust, and so on. As we focus on Christ we come to understand his will and submit our wills to it. When that happens, we bear witness to the glory he has given us (verse 22). The world sees something it can't reproduce, and people begin to thirst for the true living water of Jesus. May *you* become that kind of church/group.

8–10. Answers will vary.

mission
propelled by good news

At Serge we believe that mission begins through the gospel of Jesus Christ bringing God's grace into the lives of believers. This good news also sustains and empowers us to cross nations and cultures to bring the gospel of grace to those whom God is calling to himself.

As a cross-denominational, reformed, sending agency with more than 200 missionaries and 25 teams in 5 continents, we are always looking for people who are ready to take the next step in sharing Christ, through:

- **Short-term Teams**: One- to two-week trips oriented around serving overseas ministries while equipping the local church for mission

- **Internships:** Eight-week to nine-month opportunities to learn about missions through serving with our overseas ministry teams

- **Apprenticeships:** Intensive 12–24 month training and ministry opportunities for those discerning their call to cross-cultural ministry

- **Career:** One- to five-year appointments designed to nurture you for a lifetime of ministry

Serge Grace at the Fray   **Visit us online at: serge.org/mission**

www.newgrowthpress.com

spiritual
renewal
resources for you

Disciples who are motivated and empowered by grace to reach out to a broken world are handmade, not mass-produced. Serge intentionally grows disciples through curriculum, discipleship experiences, and training programs.

Resources for Every Stage of Growth

Serge offers grace-based, gospel-centered studies for every stage of the Christian journey. Every level of our materials focuses on essential aspects of how the Spirit transforms and motivates us through the gospel of Jesus Christ.

- **101**: The Gospel-Centered Series
  Gospel-centered studies on Christian growth, community, work, parenting, and more.

- **201**: The Gospel Transformation Series
  These studies go a step deeper into gospel transformation, involve homework and more in-depth Bible study

- **301**: The Sonship Course and Serge Individual Mentoring

Mentored Sonship

For more than 25 years Serge has been discipling ministry leaders around the world through our Sonship course to help them experience the freedom and joy of having the gospel transform every part of their lives. A personal discipler will help you apply what you are learning to the daily struggles and situations you face, as well as, model what a gospel-centered faith looks and feels like.

Discipler Training Course

Serge's Discipler Training Course helps you gain biblical understanding and practical wisdom you need to disciple others so they experience substantive, lasting growth in their lives. Available for onsite training or via distance learning, our training programs are ideal for ministry leaders, small group leaders or those seeking to grow in their ability to disciple effectively.

Serge Grace at the Fray   **Find more resources at serge.org**

resources and mentoring for every stage of
growth

Every day around the world, Serge teams help people develop and deepen a living, breathing, growing relationship with Jesus. We help people connect with God in ways that are genuinely grace-motivated and increase desire and ability to reach out to others. No matter where you are along the way, we have a series that is right for you.

101: The *Gospel-Centered* Series

Our *Gospel-Centered* series is simple, deep, and transformative. Each *Gospel-Centered* lesson features an easy-to-read article and provides challenging discussion questions and application questions. Best of all, no outside preparation on the part of the participants is needed! They are perfect for small groups, those who are seeking to develop "gospel DNA" in their organizations and leaders, and contexts where people are still wrestling with what it means to follow Jesus.

201: The *Gospel Transformation* Series

Our *Gospel Transformation* studies take the themes introduced in our 101-level materials and expand and deepen them. Designed for those seeking to grow through directly studying Scripture each *Gospel Transformation* lesson helps participants grow in the way they understand and experience God's grace. Ideal for small groups, individuals who are ready for more, and one-on-one mentoring, *Gospel Identity*, *Gospel Growth*, and *Gospel Love* provide substantive material, in easy-to-use, manageable sized studies.

The *Sonship* Course and Individual Mentoring from Serge

Developed for use with our own missionaries and used for over 25 years with thousands of Christian leaders in every corner of the world, Sonship sets the standard for whole-person, life transformation through the gospel. Designed to be used with a mentor, or in groups ready for a high investment with each other, each lesson focuses on the type of "inductive heart study" that brings about change from the inside out.

$\mathcal{Serge}$ Grace at the Fray

Visit us online at serge.org